Friend for the Journey

Joseph Moore

Friend for the Journey:
A Peer Ministry Training Program for Teens

(Youth Edition)

ST. ANTHONY MESSENGER PRESS
Cincinnati, Ohio

Nihil Obstat:

Nicholas Lohkamp, O.F.M.
Rev. Robert L. Hagedorn

Imprimi Potest:

John Bok, O.F.M.
Provincial

Imprimatur:

Most Reverend Carl K. Moeddel
Archdiocese of Cincinnati
December 6, 1993

The *nihil obstat* and *imprimatur* are a declaration that a book is considered to be free from doctrinal or moral error. It is not implied that those who have granted the *nihil obstat* and *imprimatur* agree with the contents, opinions or statements expressed.

The excerpt from *Letters to a Young Poet* by Rainer Maria Rilke, trans. by M. D. Herter Norton, copyright ©1954 by W. W. Norton and Co., Inc., is used with permission of the publisher.

Cover and book design by
Julie Lonneman

Cover photographs by
Jean-Claude LeJeune

ISBN 0-86716-211-2

©1994, Joseph Moore
All rights reserved.

Published by St. Anthony Messenger Press

Printed in the U.S.A.

Preface

Peer ministry can be described most simply as one young person helping another. The positive peer influence that occurs naturally can be nourished and enhanced and can become a source of energy for the entire community. Ministry should be authentic, spontaneous and beyond the boundaries of any formal ministry program, but formal structures offer training in the skills needed for ministry and support for those ministering to others.

Friend for the Journey teaches fundamental skills of living: good listening, communication and helping in difficult situations, most often by referring peers to agencies which can intervene effectively. While the program includes training in basic helping skills and crisis intervention, it in no way qualifies you as peer "counselors."

Throughout this training program, you will be learning more about these skills and about peer ministry through reflections, activities and hands-on experience. You will grow in confidence and learn new ways of walking with others on their journey through life.

Contents

Preface v

Part One:	Milestones on My Journey 2
Building the Team 1	My Mirror 3
	My Family Network 4
	Faith Spectrum 5
	Gifts for Ministry 6
Part Two:	Jesus, Model of Ministry 7
The Meaning of Ministry 7	More Scriptural Roots of Ministry 10
	Compassion and Self-Awareness 12
	Self-Insight 13
	Giftedness 17

Part Three:

Essential Training Modules for Skill Building 21

The Theory of Helping Skills   21

Nonverbal Communication   24

Active Listening   26

Barriers to Good Listening   29

Responding Skills   31

Questioning Skills   34

Focusing on Feelings   37

Feedback and Role-Playing   44

Conversing With a Stranger   45

Decision-Making and Problem-Solving   47

Saying No: Refusal Skills   51

How to Be a Group Leader   53

Guidelines for Preparing a Talk   57

Ethical Standards and Confidentiality   59

A Twenty-Four Hour Leadership Workshop   62

Part Four:

Crisis Intervention 65

Fundamentals of Crisis Intervention   65

Alcohol and Other Drugs   66

Pregnancy, Abortion and Sexual Activity   71

Abuse   74

Eating Disorders   77

Divorce and Blended Families   78

Death and Loss   82

HIV Infection/AIDS   85

Runaways   86

Suicide   88

Part One: Building the Team

This section includes five activities for group discussion and sharing:

    Milestones on My Journey
    My Mirror
    My Family Network
    Faith Spectrum
    Gifts for Ministry

Through these exercises your peer ministry group can discover a deeper level of communication that will help you bond as a group. Forming a cohesive team is essential before learning helping skills or engaging in ministry.

Milestones on My Journey

Think back over your life from very early childhood until now. What major events have affected your life and shaped who you are today? Take several minutes to think about this question and then fill in at least four of the six "milestones" below.

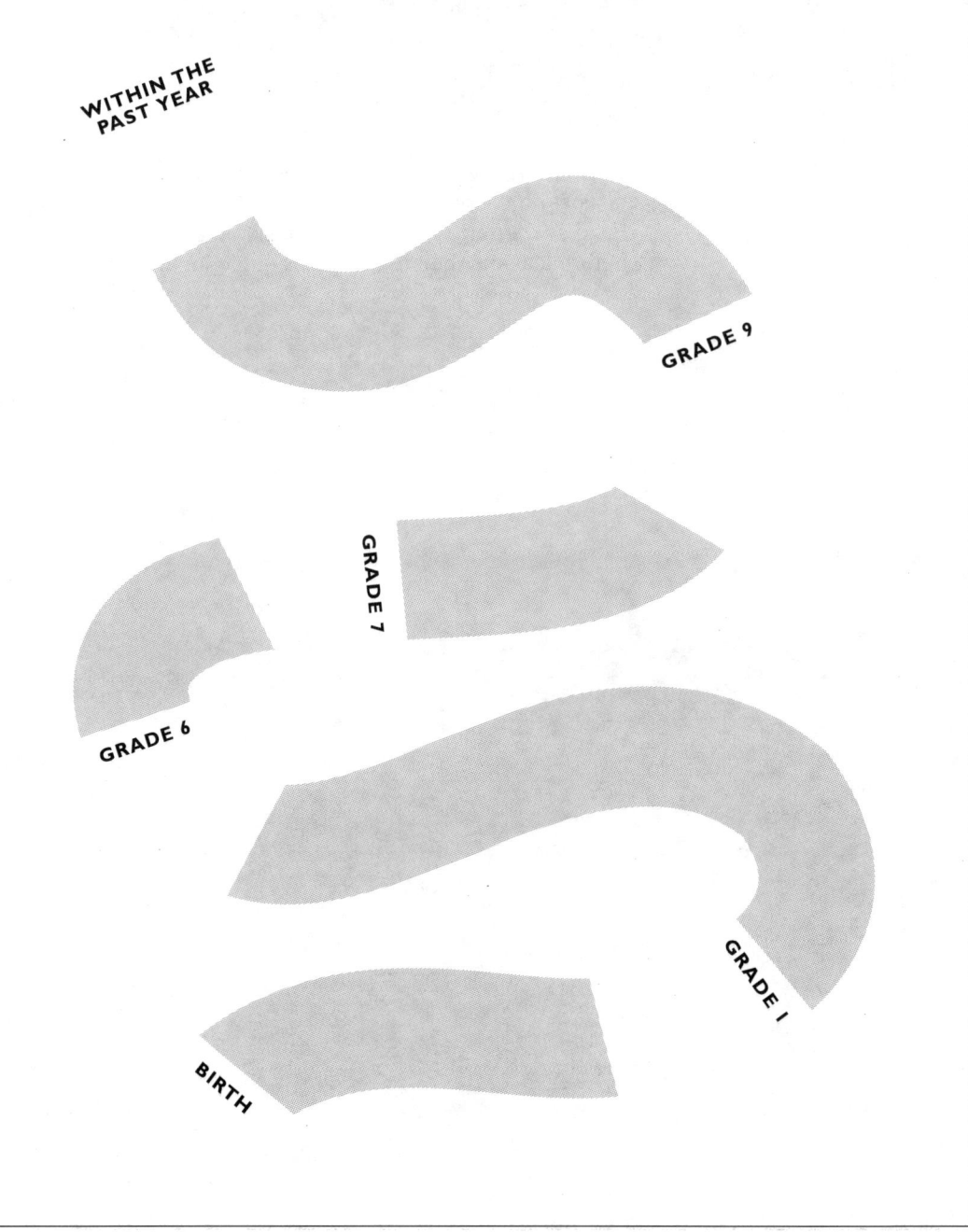

My Mirror

Complete the following sections of your mirror as honestly as possible.

A way that I act in front of others that really isn't me...	What my parents don't see in me or realize about me...
The type of kid society (my friends, teachers, classmates, people I work with) sees me as...	The best way to describe who I really am...

My Family Network

In the circle nearest to "me" put the member(s) of your family closest to you; in the farthest, the person who is the farthest. If a person is growing closer to you and vice versa, draw an arrow from that person's name to "me." If distance is growing between you, draw an arrow from that person's name away from "me."

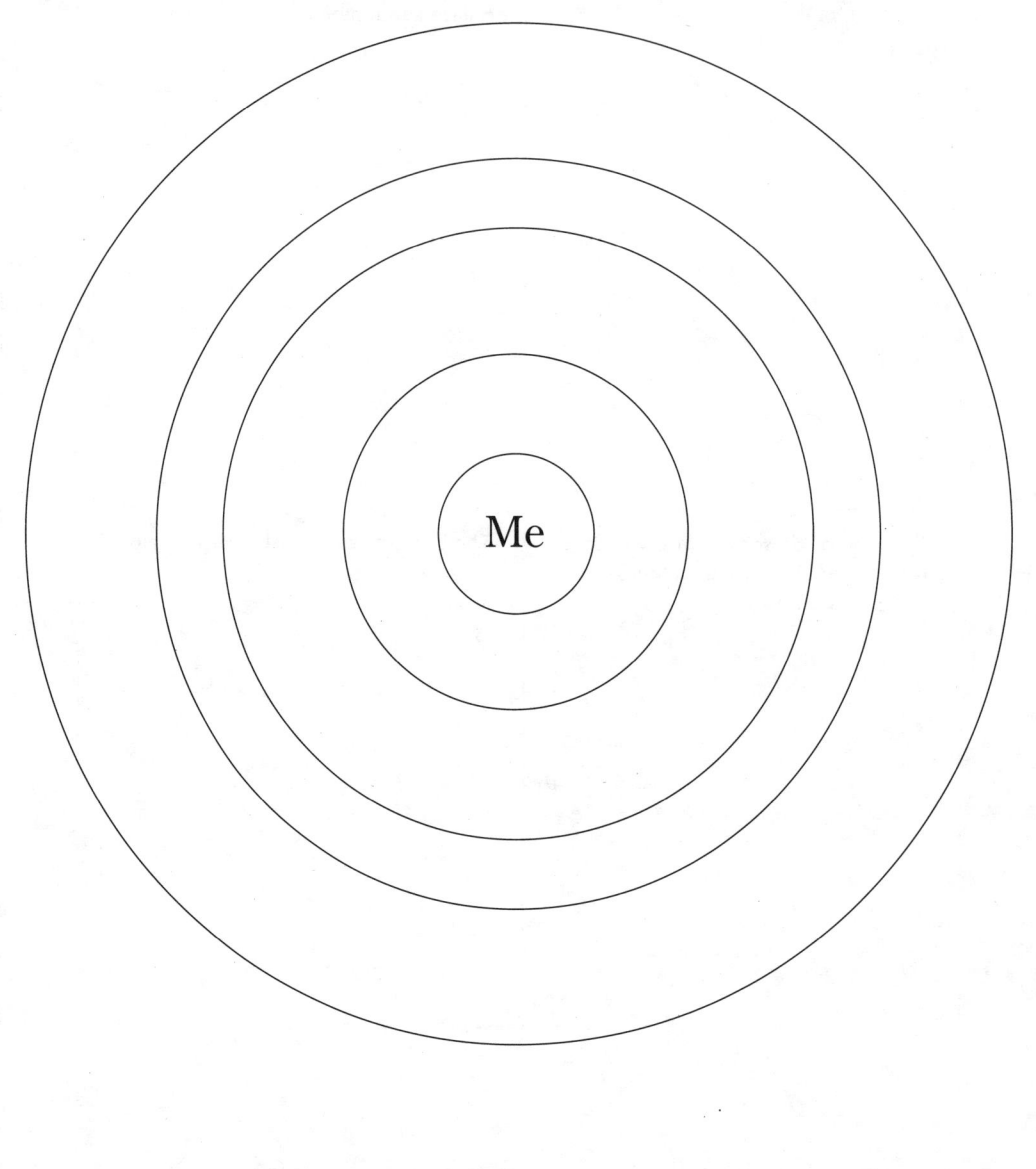

Faith Spectrum

Place yourself on the spectrum expressing nearness to or distance from God or Jesus. In the spaces below list three reasons explaining your choice of placement.

Jesus/God

1. _____

   _____

2. _____

   _____

3. _____

   _____

Gifts for Ministry

You have completed four activity sheets with your group. You have probably learned a good deal about each other and made some observations about each group member. In the spaces below list each person in your group and at least one positive aspect you see in his or her personality, things you consider strong points for a peer minister to possess. When you share your observations, feel free not only to name the positive point, but to elaborate on it, taking the time to affirm each other.

       Name   Positive Quality

1. _____   _____

2. _____   _____

3. _____   _____

4. _____   _____

5. _____   _____

6. _____   _____

7. _____   _____

8. _____   _____

9. _____   _____

10. _____   _____

11. _____   _____

12. _____   _____

(add more names if necessary)

Part Two: The Meaning of Ministry

The Meaning of Ministry

Ministry is more than care, concern and altruism, although it encompasses those humanitarian realities. The word *ministry* comes from the Greek word *diakonia*, which means "serving at a table, the work of a servant or slave." The Christian community chose *diakonia* to describe the work done by its leaders and special workers. Ministry is public action on behalf of the Christian community to bring about the reign of God. Through Baptism and Confirmation, all Christians have a call to ministry. Priests in the Catholic, Anglican and Orthodox Churches, as well as ministers in Protestant Churches, participate in "ordained" ministry. We have other designated ministries in our Christian communities such as music ministry, eucharistic ministry, ministers of the word, parish council ministry and so on. A formalized peer ministry program is yet another form of designated ministry. All of these formal ministries flow out of the vocation each individual has to bring about that mysterious reality called the reign or kingdom of God, a world in which love and unselfishness create a new order.

Jesus, Model of Ministry

The entire mission of Jesus was to bring about the kingdom of God. Jesus directed his ministry to his peers, his apostles and disciples. He taught them through his words but even more through his example. What can we learn about peer ministry by observing Jesus in the Gospels?

Jesus was approachable. Throughout his public life, Jesus allowed anyone to approach him, even those who were blind or lame or outcast by Jewish society. Luke even tells us that he healed a woman who tugged at his clothing (Luke 8:45). In other words, he didn't send out signals that said: "Don't bother me" or "Mind your own business." He had an inner openness that must have been expressed in the way he looked at and greeted others. How about you? Do you say "hi" to other kids in school, even those you don't know? Do you smile at strangers in church or in a checkout line at a store? Do you look people in the eye as opposed to keeping your eyes downcast? The initial signals we send to our peers are crucial in letting them know whether or not we are open and approachable.

Jesus was nonjudgmental. Jesus disregarded the social status of the people he met. Tax collectors were despised by the Jews because they worked for the unpopular Roman government, yet Jesus associated with them. He also spoke with adulterers and people with various diseases that were considered to be curses sent from God. He ate with the rich and poor, the educated and the ignorant. People often quote the American humorist Will Rogers as saying, "I never met anyone I didn't like." Jesus could have said this too. It doesn't mean that he approved of every behavior that he encountered, but he didn't reject people because they had done something wrong or had a particular label. How about you? Can you accept *anybody* or do you have trouble in this area? Are there groups of people in *your* society that you make judgments about or reject?

Jesus was inclusive. Jesus' concern was universal, that is, it included everybody. Reflect on this story from the Gospel of Luke (10:29-37).

> But because [the man] was anxious to justify himself, he said to Jesus, "And who is my neighbor?" Jesus replied, "A man fell victim to robbers as he went down from Jerusalem to Jericho. They stripped him, beat him and went off leaving him half-dead. A priest happened to be going down that road, but when he saw him, he passed by on the opposite side. Likewise a Levite came to the place, and when he saw him, he passed by on the opposite side. But a Samaritan traveler who came upon him was moved with compassion at the sight. He approached the victim, poured oil and wine over his wounds and bandaged them. He then lifted him up on his own animal, took him to an inn and cared for him. The next day, he took out two silver coins and gave them to the innkeeper with the instruction, 'Take care of him. If you spend more than what I have given you, I shall repay you on my way back.' Which of these three, in your opinion, was neighbor to the robbers' victim?" He answered, "The one who treated him with mercy." Jesus said to him, "Go and do likewise."

Do reflection on page 9

In this story, Jesus answers the question "Who is my neighbor?" Samaritans and Jews hated each other, and yet a Samaritan helps a Jew in need. According to Jesus, my neighbor is everyone who crosses my path and is in need of something or someone. This story holds several profound insights. Those *expected* to help (the priest and the Levite) did not; the least likely person, the Samaritan, is the one

Reflection: The Ministry Is the Minister

In light of these three characteristics of Jesus, answer the following questions about yourself.

1. Do you think others find you:

    ☐ very approachable   ☐ usually approachable   ☐ not very approachable?

2. What type of behavior do you engage in when you don't want to be bothered by people?

    ☐ isolate yourself   ☐ pretend not to see   ☐ act like you don't care   ☐ another behavior

3. Are you a judgmental person? Do you instinctively have negative reactions to any of the groups listed below to the point that you would not want to associate with them?

    ___black people   ___males

    ___white people   ___females

    ___Asians   ___ex-convicts

    ___Native Americans   ___Republicans

    ___Hispanics   ___Democrats

    ___people living with AIDS   ___Jews

    ___old people   ___Arabs

    ___gays or lesbians   ___rich people

    ___clergy or religious   ___people on welfare

    ___police   ___people who like a certain type of music

    ___physically disabled people   ___mentally ill people

4. If you had been walking down the road to Jericho that day and saw a beaten person lying in the road, would you have stopped to help? Be honest with yourself. If you think you would have passed him by, what would your reasons have been?

who reaches out. Sometimes a young person isn't *expected* to be a minister and yet makes more of a difference than an adult. Also, sometimes victims make the best helpers. Maybe the Samaritan, being a member of a persecuted minority, could identify with the man who was attacked.

Ministry is not an organized program but a set of attitudes that lead to action. We have seen that Jesus was approachable, nonjudgmental and inclusive. The ministry *is* the minister. Who you are, *your* personality, has the most profound effect on people. By working on our own personal, spiritual and emotional development we become better ministers. Ministry isn't only about changing the world; it's also about changing ourselves so that we can become better friends for the journey.

More Scriptural Roots of Ministry

Let's look at the story of the prophet Jeremiah from the Old Testament. Scripture scholars believe that Jeremiah was a teenager when God called him to be a prophet. Jeremiah is understandably reluctant:

> "Ah Lord God!" I said,
> "I know not how to speak; I am too young."
> But the Lord answered me,
> Say not, "I am too young."
>   To whomever I send you, you shall go;
>   whatever I command you, you shall speak.
> Have no fear before them,
>   because I am with you.... (Jeremiah 1:6-8)

Biblical prophets didn't predict the future; rather, they criticized the present. When Israel, God's chosen people, went astray from God's commands, the prophets called them back to faithfulness. The prophets had to deliver an unpopular message. An example of such a prophet from our own times is the Rev. Dr. Martin Luther King, Jr., who spoke out against racism in the United States.

Do reflection on page 11

Both the Church and society need the voice of young people unwilling to settle for the status quo. Young people are often quick to recognize hypocrisy. They speak the truth as they see it. As people get older they often become more compromised by the struggles of daily living; sometimes they become cynical and lose hope. We need the freshness, the energy and the bravery of young people to help the Church and the country become all that they can be. We need people of all generations to be the people of God.

Sometimes we minister by speaking out about injustice

> **Reflection: How Daring Are You?**
>
> When you see something in the Church or in society that you really feel is wrong or unjust, do you keep it to yourself or do you speak out? When you see peers treated unjustly by other kids, do you speak up in their behalf or are you afraid?
>
> **Timidity Meter**
>
> Put a check at the place that best describes you when you believe something or someone is wrong. Do you:
>
> —always speak out
>
> —probably say something
>
> —say nothing but later tell friends
>
> —seldom say anything because you don't like others to know how you feel
>
> —never speak out

or a lack of faithfulness to God's ways in an individual or in society as a whole. Now let's look at a passage from the New Testament that shows how ministry can also be humble and quiet service.

Before the feast of Passover, Jesus knew that his hour had come to pass from this world to the Father. He loved his own in the world and he loved them to the end. The devil had already induced Judas, son of Simon the Iscariot, to hand him over. So, during supper, fully aware that the Father had put everything into his power and that he had come from God and was returning to God, he rose from supper and took off his outer garments. He took a towel and tied it around his waist. Then he poured water into a basin and began to wash the disciples' feet and dry them with the towel around his waist. He came to Simon Peter, who said to him, "Master, are you going to wash my feet?" Jesus answered, "What I am doing you do not understand now, but you will understand later." Peter said to him, "You will never wash my feet." Jesus answered him, "Unless I wash you, you will have no inheritance with me." Simon Peter said to him, "Master, then not only my feet, but my hands and head as well!" Jesus said to him, "Whoever has bathed has no need except to have his feet washed, for he is clean all over; so you are clean, but not all." For he knew who would betray him; for this reason he said, "Not all of you are clean."

So when he had washed their feet [and] put his garments back on and reclined at table again, he said to them, "Do you realize what I have done for you? You call me 'teacher' and 'master,' and rightly so, for indeed I am. If I, therefore, the master and teacher, have washed your feet, you ought to wash one another's feet. I have given you a model to follow, so that as I have done for you, you should also do." (John 13:1-15)

The task of washing feet before a meal, a custom when guests arrived from walking dusty roads in sandals, was usually performed by a household servant or slave. When Jesus washes the feet of his friends he gives us an example of humble ministry. (Remember our discussion of ministry as *diakonia*.)

So often helping others is a matter of little hidden acts of service: opening a door, taking out the trash, doing what a friend prefers, helping someone with homework. Ministry is never an elitist activity. It is never a statement that we are better than others or above others in any way. This is a subtle danger that can sometimes occur in a formal peer ministry or youth leadership program. Sometimes a group bonds so closely and achieves such great things that they can get a collective swelled head. If you feel tempted to brag about your ministry, reread this story of Jesus washing his disciples' feet.

Compassion and Self-Awareness

Compassion (from two Latin words: *co* and *patior*) literally means "to suffer with." Most ministry is simply compassion. When our friends turn to us out of their own pain, we usually cannot take their pain away. They may have a problem in the family or in a relationship. Perhaps they have been abused or the victim of discrimination. Maybe they are dealing with a death, a divorce or a drug addiction. Ninety-nine percent of the time in ministry with friends we cannot take away the pain, but we can share in it. We can *suffer with* our friends. Simply by being there we can reduce the stress, anxiety or sorrow that another feels.

To suffer with others requires a lot of self-awareness. We need to realize that we too are hurting human beings. No matter what has befallen our friends, even if their bad behavior brought on a problem, we are not a stranger to it. We may not have made exactly the same mistakes, but we recognize that we are capable of acting in destructive ways. Compassion for others is rooted in the awareness that we too suffer and struggle, that we too need the support and comfort of friends.

Realizing our woundedness awakens us to our need for emotional and spiritual healing. There is usually no quick fix for our problems, no cure, but the care we extend to each other is a genuine source of healing. It brings about the kingdom of God. Our society, so eager to find easy solutions to any discomfort, has a hard time with this concept of spiritual healing. We are so accustomed to instant remedies that we often fail to see grace in each other, even in the midst of a problem.

Self-Insight

Do the reflection on page 14

The psychological task of the teenage and young adult years is to answer the question "Who am I?" Sometimes you might feel very unsure about the answer. We have many "masks" that we wear in public. With one group of people you may act one way; with another group, another way; by yourself, different still. So which one is the real you?

It can be painful to face yourself honestly and to figure out your real goals, values and direction in life. It's easier to wear one mask after another. Some kids choose the "macho" role, the "cheerleader," the "brain," the "clown," the "cynic" or the follower of a particular type of music. Sometimes we wear a mask so often that it seems permanent. Some people don't find out until later in life who they really are. Some people may never figure it out.

How can you sort out your identity, the real you? The best way is through the experience of intimacy. Intimacy as a psychological term has nothing to do with sex. I am intimate with someone when I share with that person the deepest parts of myself. When I experience intimacy with someone, I feel free to speak about the darker side of my

Reflection: The Masks We Wear

Answer the following as best you can.

A mask I wear with my parents is...

A mask I wear in school is...

A mask I wear with my friends is...

A way I kid myself is...

> Don't be fooled by me.
> Don't be fooled by the masks I wear.
> For I wear a thousand masks, and none of them is me.
> I give the impression that I am secure.
> Confidence is my name and coolness is my game.
> But don't believe me.
> Beneath lies the real me—in confusion and fear and aloneness.
>
> But I don't tell you this, because I'm afraid.
> I am afraid that you will think less of me, that you'll laugh at me.
> I'm afraid that deep down I'm nothing and I'm no good.
>
> Yet only you can call me into aliveness.
> Each time you're kind and encouraging.
> Each time you try to understand because you care.
> Who am I, you may wonder. I am someone you know very well.
> I am every man, woman and child you meet.
>
> —Anonymous

> Who am I?... This or the other?
> Am I one person today and tomorrow another?
> Am I both at once?
>
> —From "Who am I?" by Dietrich Bonhoeffer

self—my fears, what I am ashamed of, what makes me think I must be different from others. When I trust someone enough to speak about these things, and that person accepts me in spite of what I have revealed about myself, the acceptance affirms who I am. It lets me know that it's OK to be me, just as I am.

The paradox of intimacy is that to be strong, I must first be weak. To achieve a strong sense of who I am, I must reveal my deepest weaknesses to at least one other person. If I hide my weakness, my fear, my shame and my doubts, keeping them to myself, I will never figure out that it's OK to be me. When I share these secrets I will probably also find out that I am not alone, that everybody has weaknesses, fears and doubts. Because we all wear masks it's hard to really know each other. Sometimes we think that people who keep everything bottled up inside are strong, but being able to take the risk to share is a sign of real strength.

In ministry it's important to be secure with *who* you are. It's helpful to have had at least one close friendship in which you could say anything. You will find it easier to accept others if you have accepted yourself through the experience of intimacy. People will tell you a lot of personal

Reflection: Self-Esteem Activity

This questionnaire will provide you with a little insight about how you see yourself. Try to respond without thinking through the choices. Your "gut reaction" is probably the most accurate. Be as honest as you can with yourself. Respond according to how you *probably* would act in the given situation *most* of the time.

Directions: Circle the letter of the phrase representing how you would act.

1. In school, the teacher and some students are discussing recycling, a subject you really care about. You:
   a. wait and see who else participates before speaking up.
   b. let them know what you think right away.
   c. listen to them, but don't share your own views.

2. The drama club is holding auditions for their upcoming musical. You've heard their productions are tough to get into, but you've always wanted to act. You:
   a. audition for the fun of it; you'll never make it, but at least you can say you tried.
   b. read the play and watch the movie version a few times before the audition so you can knock 'em dead when the big day arrives.
   c. sign up to audition but chicken out at the last minute.

3. You're really disappointed about not getting that spot on the basketball team, but at least it went to a classmate who deserved it. When you find yourself sitting at the same lunch table, you:
   a. don't say anything; you're too upset; you think you are such a loser and you could never be happy for him/her.
   b. congratulate him/her.
   c. congratulate him/her, saying that he/she deserved the spot and then think to yourself that you won't give up and maybe will use your talent in a different sport or activity.

4. You're at a going-away party for a friend who's moving out of state, and the host has asked everyone to say a few words about the guest of honor. You:
   a. leave the party a little early right before the speeches start.
   b. mumble "He/she's a good kid," and let the next person talk.
   c. describe all of the fun times you and your friend have had.

5. You're on a ski trip with your girlfriend/boyfriend and his/her family. You have never skied before and when it's time to hit the slopes you:
   a. head for lessons on the smallest hill; if you do well you'll try out the more difficult trails with your girlfriend/boyfriend later.
   b. spend every day on the smaller hill; you're not about to risk life and limb on a harder hill.
   c. announce that it's too cold to ski; you'll be happier inside with TV and a warm fire.

Now add your points according to how you have answered.
1. a. 2, b. 3, c. 1   **2.** a. 2, b. 3, c. 1   **3.** a. 1, b. 2, c. 3   **4.** a. 1, b. 2, c. 3   **5.** a. 3, b. 2, c. 1

12-15: You are confident, believe in yourself and are willing to take risks; you have good self-esteem. 8-12: Somewhat confident, you seem to be sure of yourself sometimes, but not all of the time. You don't want to take too many chances on things that you aren't sure about. 5-8: You appear not to believe in yourself very much. You never want to take any risks because you don't think you can do it. Your problem is that you don't really realize what great potential you have. It might be a good idea to talk with someone who can help you to see all the good inside you.

Reflection

Imagine you are looking into a mirror, not to fix your hair or to check your outfit but rather to examine your soul, the heart of yourself. Who or what do you see? How do you feel about the person you are?

"Real isn't how you are made," said the Skin Horse. "It's a thing that happens to you when a child loves you for a long, long time, not just to play with, but REALLY loves you. Then you become Real."

"Does it hurt?" asked the Rabbit.

"Sometimes," said the Skin Horse, for he was always truthful. "When you are Real you don't mind being hurt."

"Does it happen all at once, like being wound up," he asked, "or bit by bit?"

"It doesn't happen all at once," said the Skin Horse. "You become. It takes a long time. That's why it doesn't often happen to people who break easily, or have sharp edges, or who have to be carefully kept. Generally by the time you are Real, most of your hair has been loved off, and your eyes drop out and you get loose in the joints and very shabby. But these things don't matter at all, because once you are Real you can't be ugly, except to people who don't understand."

—From *The Velveteen Rabbit* by Marjorie Williams

---

stuff. In order to be able to hear it and show the person love and acceptance, you have to have been through that process yourself. In other words, to minister well to others, you have to have the experience of another ministering to you.

Giftedness

Abraham Maslow, the great psychologist, suggests that only about five percent of all people develop themselves fully. Why do so many of us fail to go after greatness or stretch ourselves to our full potential? Part of the answer lies in the way that we were brought up by our parents. Some parents affirm their children and display affection within the home. These factors help a child to grow up with a positive self-image. Other parents have difficulty affirming their children, who in turn grow up with less self-esteem. Whatever your experience with your parents, you have reached a point in your life where you can start to affirm yourself by acknowledging your own goodness and giftedness.

You are a unique creation and you have been given special qualities. As a minister, you need to feel good about

Reflection

Looking to your family or ancestry fill in the positive traits you think you have inherited.

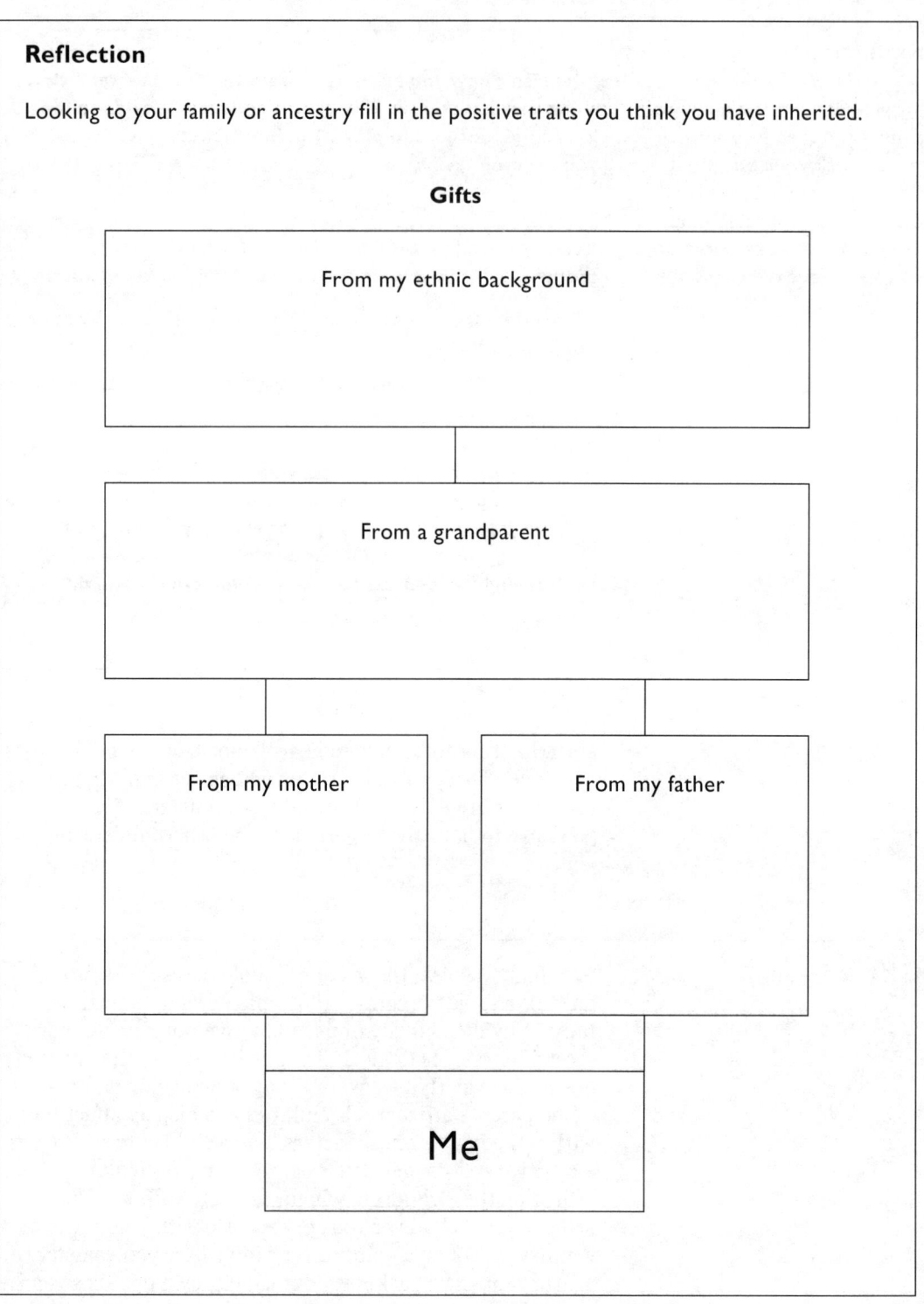

> **For me to be a saint means to be myself.**
>
> Thomas Merton, *Seeds of Contemplation*

yourself in order to help others feel good about themselves. We all like to be with people who have the inner freedom to be themselves. Part of this liberation is to recognize the God-given gifts each of us possesses. It's easy to know your faults and failures, but do you also know your good points?

Reflection

What is a good trait that other people say that you have?

What is a good trait that you see in yourself?

What gift do you possess that hasn't been developed to its full potential?

Prayer

Jesus, our model of ministry, help us to be more like you. Help us to be approachable when we feel tired or cranky or shy. Help us to be open to everybody even when feelings of prejudice come over us. Help us not to judge others. And finally, give us the strength to take the risk of ministering even when everybody else walks by the person who is hurting. Amen.

Part Three: Essential Training Modules for Skill Building

The Theory of Helping Skills

There are various theories of how to be a good helper and how people solve their problems. This program presents a theory and skills for the helper who is *not* a professional psychotherapist (like you!). Psychotherapy demands years of professional and academic training. But peer ministry isn't psychotherapy. It's simply one person helping another person to cope with the struggles of everyday life. That sounds like friendship, but neither is peer ministry friendship, because it extends beyond just our friends. It's an attitude of openness to all of our brothers and sisters. Jesus calls every Christian to this openness.

A big part of this ministry is peer helping, which means one young person reaching out to help another in the challenges and difficulties of life. The effectiveness of this *helping* part of ministry depends largely on how sincere you are and how skilled you are as a helper.

No one can provide a training course in concern and sincerity, but these training modules can help you become a more effective helper by teaching you how to be a better listener, how to support your friends in their own decision-making and problem-solving and how to intervene in serious issues like threats of suicide.

We have already discussed compassion; now we will add more attitudes and postures of a peer helper.

A peer helper is centered on the helpee. A helper focuses attention on the peer with the problem, the "helpee." The helper, caring about the helpee, accepts and attempts to understand the person. Have you ever talked seriously with somebody who wasn't paying attention to you? That's the opposite of what we're talking about!

A peer helper facilitates a conversation. A peer with a problem needs to talk it out with another *trusted* human being. When people keep their problems locked up inside, the problems usually get worse and solutions become less possible. The helper tries to get the helpee to talk by being a good listener. Most of the helping skills presented here deal with being a good listener. A good listener functions like a mirror. When I tell my problem to another person, I put it out in front of me. A good listener reflects back to me what I have just said, which enables me to see the problem more clearly. Have you ever discussed a confusing problem with a good listener and seen the issues more clearly afterward? That listener was like a mirror for you.

A peer helper refrains from giving advice. At times advice is helpful, but generally not when peers speak to you about their problems. Our theory of peer helping is that people solve their problems by talking them out with a good listener who cares, who is sincere and who attempts to understand and accept the helpee. But the choices, solutions or decisions made need to be those of the helpees. This enables the helpee to "own" the choice or decision. If you rush in and want to solve others' problems for them, you rob them of the opportunity to come to their own solution. If you impose your own solution and it fails, whose fault will it be?

A high school senior once asked me if I thought it would be better for her to wait to go to college. Kristen was an intelligent young woman who had no trouble with studies, but she wanted to do a year of volunteer work in a distant part of the country before going to school again. I had my own opinion of what *I* thought she should do, but I knew if I shared it with her it would be just as bad as giving advice. I wanted Kristen to be responsible for what she chose, and if it didn't work out I wanted her to be able to blame only herself and to learn from that failure. If she made what turned out to be a good decision, I also wanted that to be truly hers as well.

When people have problems, they usually feel confused. They don't know what to do. Our theory of helping, based on sound psychological principles, is that as people begin to verbalize their dilemmas, they begin to sort out this inner jumble of emotions and confusion. By talking with you they can get in touch with the feelings deep within themselves. These deep feelings are the sources of solutions; they provide direction for the steps to be taken. Sometimes people have to talk out a problem many times before they can reach these inner feelings and directions.

Don't be quick to provide advice early on, before people reach the point where they can give themselves that advice. Resist the temptation to rush in and take away their pain. You may care very much for someone, and it may even hurt you to see that person suffer, but your advice will be no quick fix. Remember that compassion is about being with others in their suffering; it's more about care than cure. Resist the temptation to jump in with your own advice. Even when helpees ask you for advice, gently refuse to give it, suggesting that it's better if they come to the solution on their own.

Reflection

Write a sentence summarizing the last time you went to discuss a real problem with a trusted friend or confidante.

Now ask yourself: Was it advice that you were looking for at that time? If not, what was it that you wanted from your friend?

Reflection: Could You Just Listen?

When I ask you to listen to me and you start giving me advice, you have not done what I asked.

When I ask you to listen to me and you begin to tell me why I shouldn't feel that way, you are trampling on my feelings.

When I ask you to listen to me and you feel you have to do something to solve my problem, you have failed me, strange as that may seem.

Listen! All I asked was that you listen, not talk or do—just hear me.

Advice is cheap; 35 cents will get you both Dear Abby and Billy Graham in the same paper.

I can do for myself; I'm not helpless—maybe discouraged and faltering, but not helpless.

When you do something for me that I can and need to do for myself, you contribute to my fear and inadequacy.

But when you accept as a simple fact that I do feel what I feel, no matter how irrational, then I can quit trying to convince you and can get on with the business of understanding what's behind this irrational feeling. When that's clear, the answers are obvious and I don't need advice.

Irrational feelings make more sense when we understand what's behind them.

Perhaps that's why prayer works, sometimes, for some people—because God is mute and doesn't give advice or try to fix things. God just listens and lets you work it out for yourself.

So please listen and just hear me.

And if you want to talk, wait a minute for your turn—I'll listen to you.

—Anonymous

Reflection: Your Helping Profile

Since you haven't really learned these helping skills yet, place yourself where you think you honestly fall on these lines. (A month after you have finished these training modules, it would be interesting to do this exercise again.)

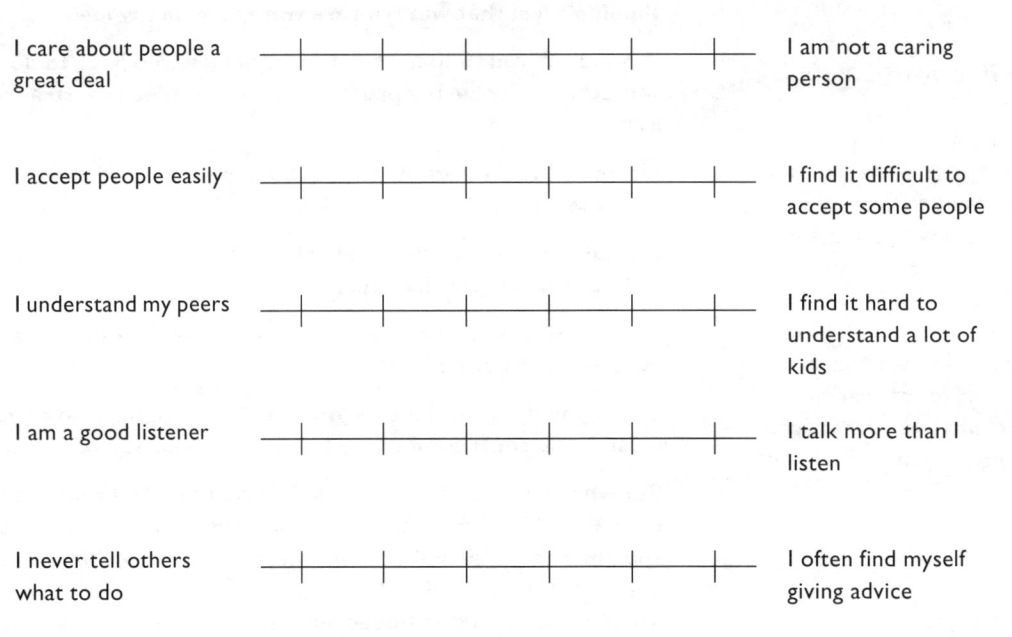

I care about people a great deal	I am not a caring person
I accept people easily	I find it difficult to accept some people
I understand my peers	I find it hard to understand a lot of kids
I am a good listener	I talk more than I listen
I never tell others what to do	I often find myself giving advice

Draw a vertical line linking the dots to find your helping profile. The further to the left your line is, the more you probably possess natural gifts to be a good helper. If your line falls more to the right, remember that helping skills can also be learned and acquired.

Nonverbal Communication

A large percentage of our communication is nonverbal: facial expressions, gestures, body language. A smile, a frown, a red flush of anger, furrowed eyebrows, a pat on the back, a handshake, a wave, a hug, the way we look at each other—these can all speak volumes. Notice your helpee's nonverbal communication. Does she continually rub her hands as she speaks, suggesting anxiety? Does he shout? Does he almost stutter? Does her facial expression change when a certain name is mentioned?

Look for the feelings *behind* the words. Have you ever said, "What's wrong?" to a friend who looks depressed, only to have him snap back "Nothing's wrong!"? Or, someone may bristle with anger but say, "No, I'm not angry at her."

In cases like this, people are often unaware of their own feelings. Their words say one thing, but their body language says something else. Sometimes nonverbals match the spoken word and sometimes they contradict it. A perceptive helper will try to notice emotions, expressions and body language as well as what is being said. This requires both practice and skill.

The Helper's Nonverbal Communication

In addition to observing your helpee's nonverbal expressions, you need to notice your own. You will find these five types of nonverbal communication helpful.

1. *Body posture.* If you slouch backward or rest your head on your arms while someone is telling you a problem, your body language says, "I don't care about your problem." You might care a lot, but the impression that you don't is significant. As a helper, it is best to sit in a chair opposite the helpee, leaning *slightly* forward toward the person. Don't fold your arms across your chest; this creates a barrier.

2. *Eye contact.* Have you ever talked to someone who kept looking away from you and smiling at other people passing by? You probably felt like this person wasn't really listening to what you were saying. You need to give the helpee the feeling that you *are* listening. Focus on the person's eyes (but don't get into a staring contest!). Look into the person's eyes with sincerity and interest. Don't look down or away.

3. *Tone of voice.* Keep your voice in a medium range. Refrain from both whispering and shouting as these behaviors could unnerve the helpee.

4. *Head movement.* An occasional slight nod of the head assures the helpee that you are truly listening; it encourages the person to keep speaking. This movement shouldn't be rapid and continuous but simply occasional.

5. *Personal habits.* A helpee will be distracted if you file your nails, scratch, adjust your clothing, twist your hair, play with a pencil, smoke, drink, tap your feet and so on. Often we aren't aware of what we are doing or how it can annoy others. Try to sit quietly and calmly as you listen to your helpee.

The activity below needs to be done with either a mirror or a partner.

Reflection: Your Nonverbal Communication

Change and contort your facial expression for each of the following emotions. Notice how your or your partner's face changes.

1. joy
2. frustration
3. thinking someone else is behaving strangely
4. peaceful
5. outraged
6. hurt feelings
7. confused
8. afraid
9. smug/satisfied with your accomplishment

Artificiality

Like learning how to ice skate or do a new dance step, many helping skills feel artificial at first. You might say: "I felt like such a fake leaning forward and nodding my head." But like any skill that feels awkward when you are trying to acquire it, it becomes second nature with practice. Once you have practiced these helping skills, they will become a part of you and kick in naturally when you sense that you are listening to a problem. Expect to feel awkward and artificial at first.

Active Listening

We think of speaking as active and listening as passive. But the prominent psychologist Carl Rogers has called listeners to an active role. To listen to people, pay attention to what is being said. Responding appropriately takes real energy. It's a skill, and a difficult one to acquire. In 1951 Dr. Rogers published *Client-centered Therapy: Its Current Practice, Implications and Theory.* His approach to helping is useful to nonprofessional helpers like peer ministers because it puts the burden for solutions on the helpee, the person with the problem. In Rogers' nondirective approach, helpers don't tell helpees how to solve their problems. Giving advice is not your role.

In addition to active listening, you are called to accept the helpees just as they are. Rogers refers to this as "unconditional positive regard," which means that the helper's attitude toward the helpee expresses no

---

A Theory of Helping Diagram

Helpee

1. The helpee needs to talk out problems in order to

2. get in touch with true feelings in order to

3. make decisions and choose paths to the solutions for problems.

The helper assists the helpee by being a good, active listener.

Active Listening Checklist

	Excellent	Fair	Poor
1. eye contact	☐	☐	☐
2. posture	☐	☐	☐
3. tone of voice	☐	☐	☐
4. nodding of head	☐	☐	☐
5. brief remarks to show the helper was paying attention	☐	☐	☐
6. focused on the speaker despite distractions	☐	☐	☐
7. kept speaker on track when wandering	☐	☐	☐
8. wasn't judgmental	☐	☐	☐

9. Did the helper have any distracting personal habits?

10. What is one way in which this helper might improve his or her listening skills?

disapproval or negative evaluation.

We mention Carl Rogers here to help you understand that the theories of helping in this program haven't just come out of thin air. For the past fifty years in the United States theories of counseling, based largely on Rogers' work, have assisted caring people who aren't professional counselors to be better helpers and better friends. While Rogers wrote for the professional field of psychotherapy, many of his ideas have been developed to apply to all human relationships. Through applications of these theories, the helper learns a set of skills that foster good relationships and good communication and help people make decisions and solve problems. Think of yourself as someone who makes meaningful conversation possible through active listening skills, which can lead others to make choices for their own well-being.

Characteristics of Active Listening

We have already discussed nonverbal skills for active listeners: eye contact, posture, tone of voice, personal habits and head movement. We have also mentioned that a good listener pays attention to the feelings underneath what is being said. Below are eight steps for active listening that summarize these skills and two more that will be discussed later.

Eight Steps for Active Listening

1. *Make eye contact* with the speaker.

2. *Focus on the speaker.* Don't just "hear" what is being said, really listen by blocking out other distractions.

3. *Listen for the feelings as well as the words being spoken.*

4. *Show that you are listening* by occasional nods of your head, and by saying "uh huh" or other short words in the course of listening. Periodically check with the speaker to make sure that you have heard correctly. For example, you might say, "So you're saying he's really changed?" If you don't grasp what the speaker means, ask a clarifying question to show that you are paying attention.

5. *Keep the speaker on track.* If she starts to get off the subject or expand on a detail unrelated to the problem, try to help her refocus on the issue she was discussing.

6. *Show acceptance.* You can do this primarily by *not* making judgments about what is being said with your facial expression or your remarks.

7. *Respond to what is being said.* (We will discuss responding skills later.)

8. *Give appropriate feedback.* (We will discuss feedback later.)

Barriers to Good Listening

Before continuing with skill development, let's examine some barriers or potential pitfalls to being a good listener.

1. *Being too emotionally involved with the helpee.* It's difficult to listen objectively to your best friend or a family member. For example, if your brother talks with you about running away from home, it's different from a freshman on a retreat day talking about the same issue. You probably have strong feelings about what your brother should or shouldn't do. If your best friend discusses the possible breakup of a romance, it is difficult to be a detached observer.

When people close to us present a problem, it's almost impossible to refrain from giving advice, at least indirectly (for example, "Well, if it were me, I would..."). If someone close to you needs to talk over a problem, suggest somebody less emotionally involved than you to help sort it out. Of course your friend can still come to you and talk for emotional support, but be honest enough to say that someone in addition to you may be needed to work on the issues and to come to some resolution.

2. *A recent (or past) similar experience.* If a friend comes to discuss her fears about a terminally ill parent's impending death and you yourself have recently dealt with the death of someone close to you, it might intensify your own pain too much to listen to this friend. Or you may be able to grieve along with your friend but not be able to offer the objective support needed to get through this crisis. You might become two helpees in need of a helper. Again, be honest enough to say that your own recent painful experience is too close to you, that this issue is too tender for you to be helpful.

A past issue could also be a barrier to good listening. For example, if a friend confides being abused to you and you yourself are a victim of abuse it may be difficult for you to be a helper.

Past similar experiences are not always a barrier; sometimes they enhance your ability to help. For instance, if your parents divorced five years ago or one of your parents is an alcoholic, these experiences might make it easier for you to relate to a helpee struggling with the trauma of divorce or a substance-abuse issue. But be self-aware enough to know whether your own past history is a help or a hindrance when someone seeks you out.

3. *Not having dealt with an issue yourself.* If you haven't faced an issue in your personal life, then you're not in a position to be a good helper to someone else dealing with

the same issue. For example, if a helper is anxious about alcoholism in her family and you haven't faced alcoholism in your own family, you will feel too threatened to be a good listener on that topic. A classic example is a peer facing a question of sexual identity. If you aren't secure in your own sexual identity, you will feel threatened by the helpee's questions and confusion.

When people train for a career in professional counseling, they often undergo therapy themselves. The best helpers are in touch with their own weaknesses and insecurities. If you've faced yourself squarely and know both the inner and outer sources of your own anxieties, you will be in much better shape to help others. If you are running from difficult issues in your own life, then you can't honestly encourage others to face their issues. The best helpers turn to others to help them in their struggles of self-identity and the search for happiness in life. You will never be perfectly whole and without problems, but good helpers are honest enough to admit their vulnerability and try to deal with things. This is as important in becoming an effective peer minister as acquiring the necessary skills.

4. *Being judgmental*. You can't help others if you judge their issues or attitudes. For example, if you look down on someone who is gay or has a drug addiction or wants to have an abortion, then you really can't help the person sort out the conflict. You can't suppress your attitudes; they will come across in subtle or not so subtle ways. This doesn't mean you need to approve of abortion, for example, in order to talk to someone who's struggling with a decision about whether to seek one. To be a good helper in no way means to let go of your moral values. But just as Jesus never condemned sinners, neither can you condemn those whose values differ from yours.

If you don't really understand addiction and believe that those who turn to drugs are weak losers, you're in no position to help them. You need to refer such matters to someone else. Say something like: "I feel too strongly about people who use drugs to be a good helper for you. For your own sake you better talk with someone else." Or you might say: "My own moral principles are so opposed to abortion that I feel uncomfortable even discussing that possibility with you. I'll be able to support you if you decide to bring this pregnancy to term, but I'm not the one with whom to discuss having an abortion."

Can you see that saying that your moral views are too strong on an issue isn't the same thing as judging a person? People were drawn to Jesus because he did not judge them.

He ate with sinners and the hated tax collectors; he befriended people with leprosy and those who had committed adultery. He believed that everyone is good on the inside. He condemned sin, but never the sinner.

5. *Knowing the solution.* Sometimes two people have similar problems, but similar solutions do not work for both. If you have dealt with alcoholism in your family by joining Alateen or you have dealt with abuse by leaving home or you have dealt with divorce by going to family counseling, and these coping mechanisms have been sources of grace and strength for you, you may be too married to your own solutions to help someone with a similar problem. Your helpee *may* simply need extra encouragement from you to find the strength to go to Alateen, leave home, go to counseling or whatever, but be cautious. Your advice may not be followed. Your helpee might have tried the same solution and it failed. It might not work for your helpee the same way it worked for you.

Be aware of the great temptation to say (or even think): "I know just what you should do." You don't. You are not the other person and none of us experiences reality in exactly the same way. Even indirect attempts to offer advice can be well-meaning but not helpful: "Have you ever thought of...?" "Maybe you should try...." "What I did when I had your problem was to...." Remember that people need to arrive at their own decisions about what steps to take toward solving their problems. You can be a wonderful sounding board as they articulate alternatives.

Don't rob your helpee of the freedom to take or not take action. If someone decides on an alternative you think is right for them or you know has worked for you or for others, then of course affirm and encourage them in their resolve. But don't assume you know what others should do to find peace and happiness in life, because you don't. If you do this you will make many mistakes in your attempts to be a good helper.

Responding Skills

While we spend most of our time as helpers listening to others, we also respond to what is being said. We have already talked about *not* responding with advice or with judgments. We will discuss some ways to respond that will help others seek solutions to their problems.

"Summary statements" can be effective. They can be divided into three types:

Reflection: Judgment Sheet

Check any group of people you find it difficult to accept or have preconceived ideas about. After completion discuss your feelings with your group.

☐ pregnant teenagers	☐ shoplifters
☐ smart kids	☐ people who attempted suicide
☐ jocks	☐ people who had abortions
☐ artistic kids	☐ certain nationalities
☐ homosexuals	☐ certain ethnic or racial groups
☐ drug addicts	☐ people who are religious
☐ kids who drink	☐ teens who like a certain type of music

Is there any type of kid or any type of problem that as a helper you would be judgmental about?

Basic summary response. The helper interjects a brief phrase or word at intervals in the conversation, often accompanied by a nod of the head. This response says: "I understand what you have said so far and I encourage you to keep on speaking." Examples of basic summary statements are: "uh huh," "sure," "OK," "I see," "yes," "really," "mm hmm." We need to let the helpee know that we are truly listening. Complete silence may create tension if the helpee wonders if we are really listening or if we understand the issue. Our basic responses reassure the helpee. These responses are especially crucial when the helpee is having a difficult time opening up to you.

Summary-of-content responses. We have already discussed the role of the helper as a mirror. Helpees see their problems more clearly when they attempt to verbalize them to a good listener. Haven't you experienced greater understanding of a problem once you opened up to someone about it? As a helper you can further reflect an image of the problem to a helpee simply by summarizing what you have heard.

If the helpee says: "I got up late so I had to skip breakfast, and then I was late for school so I got a detention, which put me in a nasty mood."

Helper responds: "Sounds like your day got off to a bad start."

If the helpee says: "I'm going out Friday night, and I

work all day Saturday, and Saturday night is my brother's birthday. On Sunday I have church and catching up on my homework."

Helper responds: "So you're saying you have a pretty busy weekend."

In summary-of-content responses the helper concisely sums up what the helpee has said and reflects it. These responses keep the helpee focused and offer reassurance that you are really making an effort to understand what is being said.

Here are some ways to begin a summary of content response:

> "In other words…"
> "I hear you saying that…"
> "So you mean…"
> "What's coming across to me is…"
> "From what you've said it seems…"

3. *Summary-of-feeling response.* This is the most skillful response. By summarizing feelings, the helper can lead the helpee to increased self-awareness. This response goes beyond the words you hear to the feelings behind the words. The helper names the feelings he observes in the helpee whether the helpee has stated them or not. Remember that our theory of helping says that people with problems need to talk in order to get in touch with their feelings.

Believe it or not, we are often unclear about our feelings. A classic example is a young woman who is abused by her boyfriend and yet feels love for him. We can be very confused about what we feel and that confusion can prevent us from making good decisions and choosing good solutions. A skillful helper will try, as often as possible, to mirror to the helpee the feeling, the emotion that is observed. Even if the helper makes a mistake in naming the emotion, it's still helpful because it offers the helpee a chance to further clarify what he or she feels. For example, a helpee might say, "No, I don't feel anger as much as disappointment."

Examples

1) Helpee: Every time my brother does something wrong my father just brushes it off, but when I do something wrong I get grounded.

    Helper: Sounds like you feel a little persecuted.

2) Helpee: She has the prettiest smile, the most expensive clothes and every boy in school wants to

ask her out. And then there's me.

Helper: You seem to be feeling kind of inferior.

3) Helpee: My grandmother passed away a year ago today. I hate October when all the flowers and leaves are dying.

Helper: I hear you saying that you're feeling kind of sad right now.

Notice that the helper didn't summarize the content but rather the feeling. One response could contain a summary of both content and feeling; for example, in #3 the helper could have responded: "So October isn't a month filled with good memories for you and you're feeling kind of sad." Note how both content and feeling are summarized in one statement.

Reflecting on a person's feelings is a helpful response and requires real attentiveness to what is being said. Don't worry about stating the obvious because what is obvious to you as a helper may not be obvious to the helpee. People in our society struggle with expressing feelings and males especially have more of a problem because of their upbringing.

Questioning Skills

One obvious way to express interest in what another person says is to ask questions that encourage elaboration. But even though questions are a natural response, there is a skill involved in posing helpful questions. First, let's look at some *unhelpful* methods of questioning.

Nosiness. Questioning ultimately assists helpees in clarifying their own feelings. If you don't fully understand the situation, you may need more information in order to listen well. For example, a helpee may say: "And as soon as we got back from vacation my mother went into her old mood again and I've been miserable ever since. I even hate to be at home." In order for you to grasp the problem you need more elaboration on what "her old mood" really means. A skillful question could lead to this response: "Oh, she yells at my father all the time because she thinks he isn't looking hard enough for a job and she yells at me and my sister whenever we ask her for money. I guess underneath she's just worried about our finances, but she never says that. She just gets really irritable all the time."

Do you see that you now have a clearer picture of the issue? Your question was important. But nosiness comes in when you ask the "soap opera" details that you don't need to know to grasp the problem. For example: "Was your father fired or laid off?" "How much money did your father make anyway?" "How could you go away on a vacation when your family is hurting for money?" These kinds of questions simply seek to satisfy your own curiosity and are of no use to the helpee. Distinguish between necessary inquiry and nosiness.

Asking "why?" In general a question that begins with *why* isn't useful in a helping relationship. Think of a teacher asking, "Why didn't you finish that assignment?" or a parent asking, "Why did you stop there after school?" or a friend asking, "Why don't you like her?" These questions demand an explanation and put us at least somewhat on the defensive. Asking questions should enable helpees to clarify their feelings. If they need to defend themselves in some way, it implies that you are making a judgment. None of us chooses to confide our problems to a judgmental person; we look for someone who can accept us.

Judgments disguised as questions. A third inappropriate way to question is to make a judgment in a question form. For example: "You don't really want to do that, do you?" "You aren't going to the prom with him, are you?" "You don't really think you can win in that situation, do you?" In questions like these, you are giving your own viewpoint, which is an indirect method of advice-giving.

Closed questions. These questions can only be answered by a "yes" or "no." Recall that we are trying to get the helpee to talk more, not less, about a problem. Closed questions cut off further conversation. The opposite of a closed question is an open question, which we will explain next. Compare these two questioning styles:

Closed	**Open**
Do you like school?	How is school for you?
Are you afraid of him?	Suppose that happened again, how would you react?
Did you feel inferior to other children when you were younger?	How did you feel around other children when you were younger?

Helper's Checklist

This checklist is to be used by the obsever in the triad group activity.

	Excellent	Fair	Poor
1. eye contact	☐	☐	☐
2. posture	☐	☐	☐
3. tone of voice	☐	☐	☐
4. nodding of head	☐	☐	☐
5. brief remarks to show he/she paying attention	☐	☐	☐
6. focused on the speaker, not distracted	☐	☐	☐
7. wasn't judgmental	☐	☐	☐
8. no distracting personal habits	☐	☐	☐
9. wasn't nosy	☐	☐	☐
10. didn't ask "why" unnecessarily	☐	☐	☐

Put a check for every time you observed the following:

1. speaker got off track and helper refocused him/her
2. used a "summary-of-content" response
3. used a "summary-of-feeling" response
4. asked an open question

5. What is one way this helper could improve these skills?

Closed questions can be necessary at times, particularly at the initial information-gathering stage, but they do little to aid the helpee in clarifying the problem.

Open Questions

Like summarizing responses, questioning is a skill that helps people get in touch with their feelings. Remember that the discovery of how I really and deeply feel about something is the first step in making a decision or solving my problem. Open questions invite the helpee to speak more about the problem. They also probe more deeply to unlock feelings the helpee may not have noticed. Have you ever not realized how angry you were about something until someone began to ask you what happened? A question causes you to verbalize, and by doing so you begin to discover the angry feelings beneath the surface.

Jack came to talk with me about how he was no longer getting along with his best friend. He said he felt guilty about it and often regretful, but he couldn't seem to stop being irritated with his best buddy. As I asked a series of open questions such as "How do you feel when out with him at a party?" Jack discovered layers of jealousy within himself that he didn't even realize were there before we started talking. His friend had found a really sweet girlfriend, and Jack was resentful of the time she took up. He was also envious that his friend had found a girl and he hadn't. I had done very little except to invite Jack to tell me more about his friendship and the feelings surrounding it.

Focusing on Feelings

Our culture is not accustomed to talking much about feelings. How many times do we respond only to the content of what is being said and not the feelings beneath the words? Many of us find it scary to go into the feeling realm. We are more comfortable with ideas and superficial conversation in many cases. And yet no dimension of our being can be more powerful than our feelings! Being out of touch with our feelings is the source of many emotional problems.

Your helpees will come to trust you enough to talk about their feelings. Your responses and questions can help them get in touch with their own emotions. When you detect an emotion beneath the statements of a helpee, try to name that emotion as precisely as possible. In other words, it might be more accurate to say: "You sound really ticked off" than it would be to say "You sound angry." Or it

Reflection

All human emotions can be reduced to four basic ones: mad, glad, sad and scared. Try to list as many words as you can for each of these emotions. (In a group, brainstorm together using four large pieces of newsprint.)

Mad	Glad	Sad	Scared

might be more helpful to name a feeling as "bitter" than "offended"; "terrified" rather than "afraid"; "elated" rather than "happy." The more you can define a feeling, the more you reflect to a helpee what you observe. Recall that even a a mistaken description of a feeling presents the helpee with the opportunity to clarify the feeling. ("No, I don't feel so much hurt by him as I feel humiliated by what he said.")

Here are some words that attempt to pinpoint feelings.

Some 'Feeling' Words

accepted	furious	protective
afraid	glad	puzzled
annoyed	guilty	rejected
ashamed	helpless	relieved
awed	heroic	resentful
bewildered	high	restless
bitter	hopeful	sad
bored	hostile	shaky
calm	humiliated	shy
concerned	hurt	silly
confused	inadequate	subdued
defeated	indignant	sure
defensive	inhibited	tender
dejected	intense	tense
depressed	intimidated	terrified
detached	irritable	tight
disappointed	joyful	tired
disgusted	lonely	torn
eager	lost	trapped
ecstatic	miserable	ugly
edgy	morose	uneasy
elated	needy	uptight
embarrassed	neglected	vulnerable
excited	nervous	warm
fearful	passionate	weak
foolish	peaceful	worn out
free	playful	worried
frustrated	pressured	

Sabotaging Feelings

If we find it difficult to deal with our own feelings, we will also have trouble accepting others' feelings. The following list suggests ways that helpers might get in the way of helpees dealing with their feelings.

Expressing shock. Even if you are surprised at information confided to you, try to conceal that surprise as much as possible. Don't shriek, "You did what?!" Shock is a form of judgment and will send helpees the message that they have made a mistake in opening up to you.

Denying the feeling. When a helpee expresses a feeling ("Sometimes I feel like killing my father") and you deny the feeling ("You would never want to kill your father"), you are telling the helpee that it is not OK to feel what he or she feels. This is very wrong in a helping relationship. We feel what we feel; we can't help it. Feelings have no morality. They are neither right nor wrong. It's what we do with our feelings that becomes a moral issue. If I feel intense anger or jealousy or sexual attraction, it does no good at all to repress these feelings and deny they exist. It is far more healthy to admit them to myself and another person. When I can talk about the hatred I feel toward my father, for example, I can gain control of the feeling rather than let it overpower me. When a feeling is expressed, don't deny it out of your own insecurity and uneasiness with your own feelings. Allow it to be named.

Preaching, moralizing and "should-ing." Akin to denial is the attempt to preach to helpees about why they should not have this feeling. To say they "shouldn't feel that way" is irrelevant. The fact is they do! "Your father tries. You shouldn't be so hard on him." Preaching diminishes the helpees' right to feel what they feel. Never, never tell other people what they should or should not feel.

Reassuring with cliches. Have you ever expressed a sad feeling only to have it dismissed by a silly cliche that only intensifies your pain? For example, you may feel heartbroken at the end of a romantic relationship and your parent says, "Well, there are more fish in the sea" or "You'll get over it" or "Tomorrow's another day" or "It wasn't meant to be." These facile remarks and cliches say to you "I really don't want to hear what you are feeling" or "I consider this matter to be so trivial that your feelings about it are meaningless to me." Often we use cliches because we don't know what to say. For example, we may respond to a death by saying, "He's in a better place now." Cliches never comfort. They only trivialize or deny feelings or attempt to mask our own insecurity. Never respond to a helpee's feeling with a cliche.

Lecturing. It is extremely unhelpful to give your helpee a lecture using facts and logic to dismiss feelings. For example: "You shouldn't hate your father because you know that he loves you. Look at how hard he works for your family. And after all he *is* your father." The helpee already knows these things, but at the moment she still feels what she feels. Lecturing denies the reality of her emotion.

Making light of feelings. Don't make the mistake of kidding the helpee or dismissing feelings in a joking way. This says you do not take the helpee seriously.

Warning or threatening. Don't tell helpees that if they feel that way some terrible consequence will befall them. ("If you stay angry at your father, you're going to feel terrible when he dies.") Again, warnings are unnecessary, unhelpful and don't relate to the issue at hand.

Suppressing. When we suppress feelings (for example, saying, "don't cry"), we tell helpees directly or indirectly that they are not allowed to express a feeling in front of us. If they cry, allow it; if they scream, allow it; if they jump for joy, allow it. Expressing feelings in an appropriate way is the healthiest thing in the world. If you ask helpees to suppress expressions of their feelings, you betray your own lack of comfort with emotion.

Negating. When someone expresses a feeling, especially sorrow, allow it to be. Don't jump in with words right away. If the helpee cries, offer him a tissue and allow him to sniffle for a few moments in silence until he regains enough composure to speak again. If you yourself are uncomfortable with feelings, you will feel awkward and tend to want to negate the feeling by jumping in with a statement or question. Allow the emotion to be expressed.

Comparing. Don't compare what a helpee feels to someone else's feelings in the same or a similar situation. ("Well, I don't think anyone else in your family hates your father.")

Reflection

What are some unhelpful cliches and useless remarks that should be avoided in a helping relationship? List as many as you can. (In a group, brainstorm using large sheets of newsprint.)

Reflection: Clarifying Feelings

Write a *feeling* statement for each of the following. *Example*: Helpee: "My best friend ignores me now in the cafeteria." Helper: "That must really hurt."

1. Helpee: "My father and mother are fighting constantly."
   Helper:

2. Helpee: "My brother almost overdosed last weekend."
   Helper:

3. Helpee: "The cutest boy in school asked me to the prom."
   Helper:

4. Helpee: "When I look in the mirror I hate what I see."
   Helper:

5. Helpee: "That teacher never calls on me in class."
   Helper:

6. Helpee: "My father will kill me when he finds out."
   Helper:

7. Helpee: "Everyone knows what they're doing after graduation, but I don't."
   Helper:

8. Helpee: "I did it! I made the team after all."
   Helper:

Feedback and Role-playing

Feedback, in a psychological sense, means to offer another person information about how he or she is coming across to you. It isn't the same as making a judgment or telling people that they are bad or wrong. It is rather the honest sharing of your perceptions of a person's behavior. Some examples are:

> "When you make statements like that, it seems to me that your house must be more difficult to live in than my house."

> "When I see you in school and you look the other way, it makes me wonder if you are ashamed of knowing me."

Can you see that in these statements no blame is assessed, no advice is given? As a helper, you may need to provide your helpee with some challenging feedback. If you serve as a group leader, you may need to give feedback to one member of the group or to the group as a whole. For example:

> "Since only a few of you have talked during the last half hour, I'm feeling that either this topic is boring to you or else it's too threatening to discuss in a group. Am I correct?"

> "Johnny, you've been quiet most of the night. I'm wondering what's going on with you."

Feedback doesn't have to be challenging. It can also be affirming:

> "You look so pretty tonight; you always dress so nicely."

> "In my opinion, you have a lot of courage to deal with everything going on in your life right now."

> "I see you as somebody with a lot of feeling for other people and I admire the way you care about your friends."

Positive affirmation from one's peers can be a true source of healing for battered self-esteem. Be generous in affirming your family, your friends and your helpees. Don't ever be phony and say things you don't mean, but when you do observe good qualities in others, tell them about it.

Self-Referent Responses

People in peer ministry training often ask: "If I can relate to the problem of my helpee, should I tell her about my experience?" The answer is both yes and no. It helps a person feel less isolated, less different, less weird if she learns that you share the same issue. If your helpee has a parent who is an alcoholic, you might be able to say: "Gee, I know it's tough living with an alcoholic. I have an uncle who used to drink all the time so I have at least some idea of what you're talking about." But keep your identification brief and return the spotlight to the helpee immediately after your remark. Do not elaborate on your own experience and talk about how you handled the situation. You're not saying you know just how the helpee feels, because you don't. You're saying that you have *some understanding* of what the helpee must be going through because you have had a similar experience yourself.

Role-playing

Role-playing is a counseling technique. For example, you might play the person who is opposite you in a real life situation. Say a parent demands a distasteful early curfew. You play the role of your parent and ideally your parent would play you. The purpose of this kind of role-playing is to increase empathy, to stand in the other person's shoes for a bit. By acting out another's perspective you start to get some insight into another's words or behavior.

Reflection

Think of a disagreement you have with someone in your life. Pair off and ask a partner to play you. Explain your perspective on the issue and then you play your antagonist. Have a conversation for about five minutes. Then role-play your partner's situation.

Conversing With a Stranger

We might look at Jesus in the Gospels for a model of interacting with strangers. Examples include the story of Zacchaeus (Luke 19:1-10), the woman at the well (John 4:1-30) and the woman with a hemorrhage (Luke 8:43-48).

In his description of the Last Judgment (Matthew 25:31-40), Jesus points out that there really are no strangers for Christians because God is within everyone, especially in the hungry, the naked, the *stranger*, the sick and the imprisoned. Jesus tells us that if we have reached out to the stranger, we have reached out to him.

So who is the stranger? Let's begin by using common sense. It isn't necessary to pick up strangers hitchhiking on a highway to follow Jesus. He isn't talking about befriending those who clearly could be destructive. For us, strangers are those people right in our midst who don't belong to any group, who are new in school, who don't seem to have any friends, who are picked on by other kids.

Reflection

Answer these questions briefly in writing and then share your responses with the group.

1. Have you ever felt like a stranger? When? Where?

2. What is it within you that stands in the way of reaching out to people who are strangers?

Taking a Risk

Sometimes Jesus wants us to reach out and include everybody in our community, but we hold back out of fear. As a peer minister you are in a leadership role and you have the support of your peer ministry team. When you see a person sitting all alone, for example, in the school cafeteria, remind yourself of Jesus' challenge. Take a chance that this is a really nice kid you just haven't met yet. Maybe it's somebody who has been so put down at home or by his peers that he has no self-confidence and is very shy. Perhaps he needs people to reach out to him because he can't reach out himself. In a different scenario, when you feel inferior, perhaps to an adult or to somebody who is very popular, you may be afraid to risk speaking to this person because of your own insecurities and your fears of being rejected.

Try to talk yourself into taking the risk. The more you risk being friendly, the easier it becomes. Sometimes we're afraid of what our friends will think of us if we start talking with a person outside our group. This fear is rooted in our own insecurities. If we are sure of who we are and like ourselves well enough, we can withstand the comments or criticisms of our friends. Again we may need to remind ourselves of the challenge that Jesus offers and not dwell on what other people may think of us if we befriend a stranger. Also, real friends who share your values won't reject you for reaching out to someone who is lonely.

Reflection: Role-play

In this role-play, the scene is the school cafeteria. One person plays a student eating alone. The rest of the group eats at one table, laughing and talking, ignoring the student who is alone. After about three or four minutes one of the group decides to befriend the student who is alone. (Choose in advance the person who will reach out.)

Create your own script. It's up to you to play out your role(s) in any way you wish. For example, the rest of the group will decide how to behave toward the one who left them to befriend the stranger. The student alone will decide whether to be shy or talkative once befriended. You may want to do the same role-play more than once, even if you are only five or six in number, having people play different parts.

After the role-play, the student who was alone should tell the group how it felt to be alone while the others were together and how it felt after one of the group came over to start talking.

Decision-making and Problem-solving

Our theory of a helping relationship suggests that helpees can only solve their problems if they talk out the situation with an empathetic listener so that they can get in touch with their feelings. While this is accurate, a helpee can also tackle problem-solving (or decision-making) head on by following certain helpful steps.

The first step is to realize that we can actively choose solutions to life's problems. Some people feel paralyzed by insecurities or the fear of risks. They see themselves as spectators or passive victims. Life simply happens to them. They feel powerless. While there are dimensions of life over which we have no control, this doesn't mean that we can't control anything in life. Much unhappiness is rooted in the feeling that people have no power over their own existence.

I have a friend who is twenty-one years old and earning minimum wage. She complains to me constantly about her economic situation as if it were a life sentence. Her friends have suggested options like training for a new career, relocating to a better paying job, or becoming part of a new business. Rather than mustering up the courage to make a change in her life, she seems more content to remain in a miserable situation and complain about it. Have you ever said "I *can't* change" when the truth really is "I *won't* change"?

Sometimes people find the encouragement they need to make choices just by talking to a helper. Sometimes this

Reflection

Do you have a self-fulfilling prophecy about your own behavior or future? Jot it down here and share it with the rest of the group.

strength comes slowly after many conversations because the person has never viewed reality this way. As a helper you need to be proactive yourself. You need to realize that you have a right to choose and act, that you don't wait for life to happen to you. If you have no experience in taking charge of your own life, it will be almost impossible for you to assist a helpee to gain this power.

The concept of "self-fulfilling prophecy" is similar to feeling helpless. We send ourselves messages about what we can and cannot do. If you say "I could never do that," then you probably never will. If you say "I'll be a success in life," you probably will be. If you say "If I try to stop using drugs I'll never succeed," you probably won't. Self-fulfilling messages can be positive or negative. This theory maintains that we write the scripts for success or failure in our own minds and then we live them out. A helping relationship can enable a person to review these prophecies and wipe out some of the negative ones.

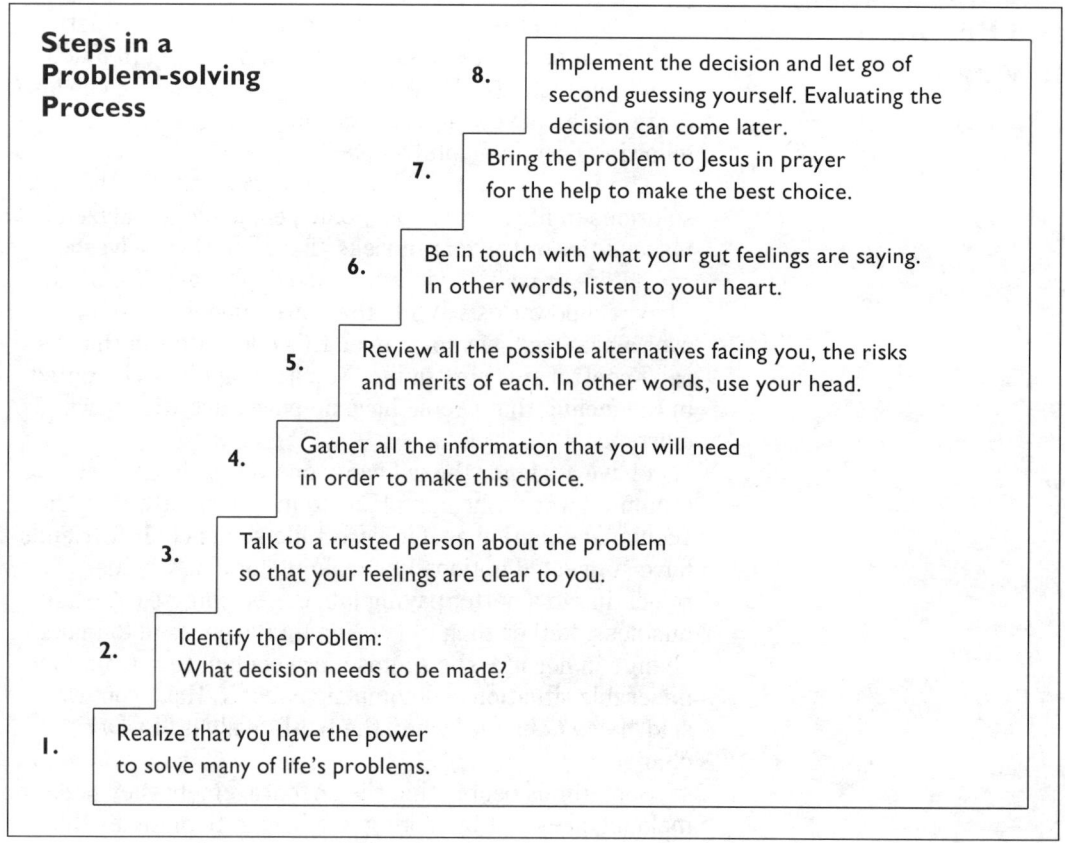

Steps in a Problem-solving Process

8. Implement the decision and let go of second guessing yourself. Evaluating the decision can come later.
7. Bring the problem to Jesus in prayer for the help to make the best choice.
6. Be in touch with what your gut feelings are saying. In other words, listen to your heart.
5. Review all the possible alternatives facing you, the risks and merits of each. In other words, use your head.
4. Gather all the information that you will need in order to make this choice.
3. Talk to a trusted person about the problem so that your feelings are clear to you.
2. Identify the problem: What decision needs to be made?
1. Realize that you have the power to solve many of life's problems.

Reflection

Have you ever made an impulsive decision based only on your feelings and then regretted it later? Share this memory of a hasty decision.

Dangers of the 'Heart'

At times we are too impatient to go through a painful problem-solving process. We want a quick fix because we are weary of a situation. We run away from home or quit our job, drop a class or end a relationship. We may need to take these actions, but we have to be sure that we have given the decision the careful deliberation the eight steps require. Otherwise we will have regrets later on. This is not to say that feelings can never be trusted, but emotions need to be tempered by reason. The combination of the two will help us make the best choices.

Dangers of the 'Head'

Sometimes people make decisions by listing the alternatives, the pros and cons, in their minds or on paper. They might come up with ten reasons for and five against. If they make their choice solely on the length of this list then they are basing it solely on reason. This discounts both the movements of the heart and the direction in which our prayer draws us.

Jesus invited the rich young man in the Gospel to follow him. From a logical standpoint it didn't make sense to the man and so he chose not to do this. But he was discounting the attraction to Jesus as well as the stirrings of his own heart because we read that the young man walked away sad. Sometimes, even though the most reasonable option has many pluses, the movement of the heart is more significant. But remember that this doesn't mean acting on impulse in order to get a quick fix.

Listen to this advice given to a young man who asks if he should become a poet, not a career that would have a long list of reasons in its favor:

> You ask whether your verses are good. You ask me. You have asked others before. You send them to magazines. You compare them with other poems, and you are disturbed when certain editors reject your efforts. Now—I beg you to give up all that. You are looking outward and that above all you should not do now—go into yourself, search for the reason that bids you to write; find out whether it is spreading out its roots in the deepest places of your heart, acknowledge to yourself whether you would have to die if it were denied you to write. This above all—ask yourself in the stillest hour of your night: Must I write? Delve into yourself for a deep answer. And if this should be affirmative, if you may meet this

earnest question with a strong and simple "I must," then build your life according to this necessity; your life even to its most indifferent and slightest hour must be a sign of this urge and testimony to it. (R. M. Rilke, *Letters to a Young Poet*, page 19.)

Negotiation

Another aspect of problem-solving is the difficulty we experience in our human relationships. The problem to be solved may be an interaction with a friend, teacher, family member, co-worker or teammate. We are going to suggest eight steps in negotiating solutions or compromises that can restore harmony to a relationship.

Sometimes people can negotiate compromises or

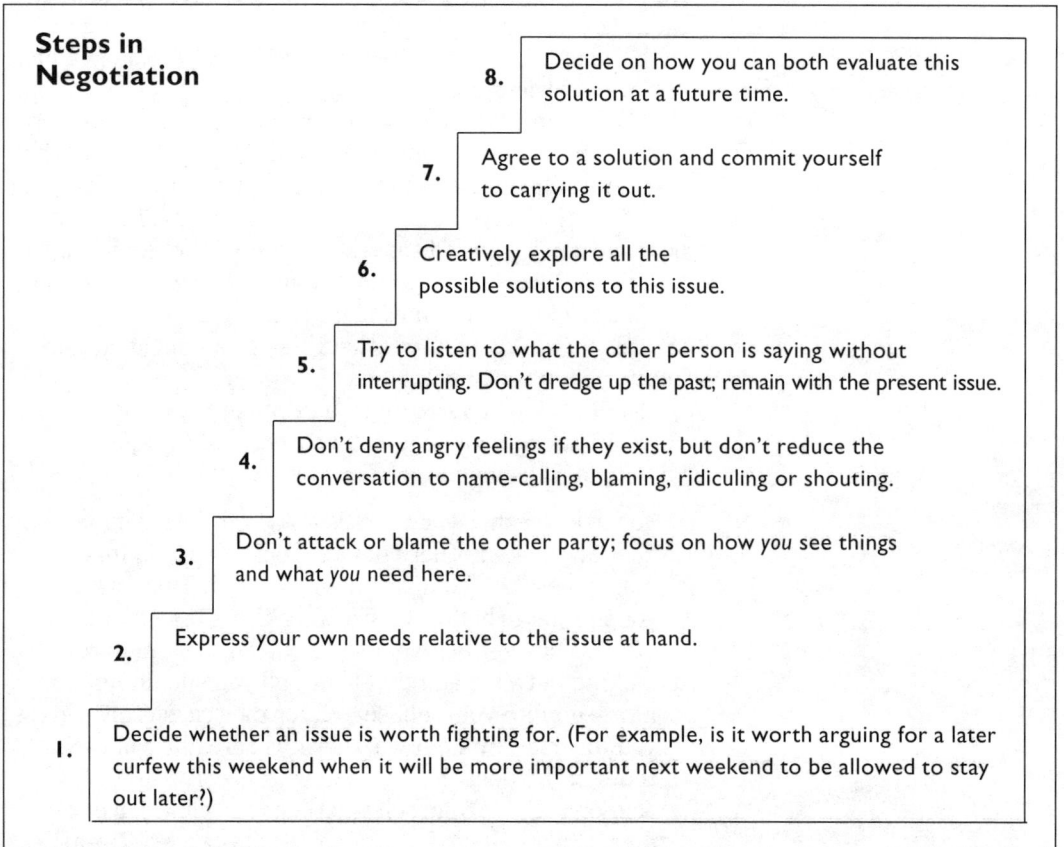

Steps in Negotiation

8. Decide on how you can both evaluate this solution at a future time.
7. Agree to a solution and commit yourself to carrying it out.
6. Creatively explore all the possible solutions to this issue.
5. Try to listen to what the other person is saying without interrupting. Don't dredge up the past; remain with the present issue.
4. Don't deny angry feelings if they exist, but don't reduce the conversation to name-calling, blaming, ridiculing or shouting.
3. Don't attack or blame the other party; focus on how *you* see things and what *you* need here.
2. Express your own needs relative to the issue at hand.
1. Decide whether an issue is worth fighting for. (For example, is it worth arguing for a later curfew this weekend when it will be more important next weekend to be allowed to stay out later?)

solutions independently and sometimes it's helpful to have a third party to keep everybody honest and to prevent the conversation from degenerating into an argument. As a helper you might be asked to assist in a negotiation, for example, between two friends or between a parent and child.

Saying No: Refusal Skills

Abraham Maslow has identified five tiers of human needs in *Toward a Psychology of Being* (2nd ed., Van Nostrand-Reinhold, New York, 1968):

When one level of need has not been met, it is very difficult, if not impossible, to move to the next step. For example, if I don't have enough to eat, I won't be concerned with my self-esteem needs; I'll be concerned about getting food. When my needs remain unmet I am likely to engage in behaviors that seem like quick ways to get what I need but are ultimately self-destructive.

For example, if I am without food or shelter I might steal or sell my body on the street or hurt someone else to take what they have. If I feel unaccepted and unloved I may try to please everyone at my own expense, allow people to make unjust demands on me and take advantage of me. If I have little self-esteem I might be tempted to cheat in order to gain recognition or lie about something or allow others to use me for their own sexual pleasure.

To some degree, we all have unmet needs and are vulnerable in some areas. It's very important to be self-aware enough to recognize these weaknesses before we get caught in a self-destructive trap. Neediness makes it difficult to say no. For example, a young woman may become pregnant in her early teens not because she has a powerful sex drive, not because she has no moral values, not because she doesn't know how to prevent a pregnancy, but because either consciously or unconsciously she thinks that her boyfriend will love her for allowing him to have sex with her or she thinks that having her own baby will mean that at least somebody in this world will love her.

The Skill of Saying No

Peer pressure either plays upon your own needs and limitations or else entices you toward peer acceptance and the promise of "a good time." Let's examine some steps that might help you resist peer pressure.

1. Recognize that you have the right to say no to engaging in behaviors you do not choose.
2. If possible, be self-aware enough not to put yourself into situations where your powers to refuse will be tested. Having good friends who share your values will also help here.
3. Name the problem and its consequences. (For example, "If I go to that party everyone will be drinking and I don't want to have that pressure on me.")
4. Explore other options. ("Why don't you go to...instead?")
5. Ultimately state what *you* intend to do and remain firm in your resolve. (For example, "Well, then why don't you drop me at home on your way to the party because I'm just not going.")

No is no; it isn't yes. There is a myth among some males that when a woman refuses a sexual advance, no means yes. Some males mistake a female's need for affection as permission for sex. The best behavior for uninvited sexual advances (whether male on female or female on male) is to be very clear in the early stages before physiological changes intensify desire. Young people need enough self-respect and enough sense of their own power to be able to refuse whatever they wish to refuse. You can grow in this skill if you continue to befriend yourself and your own best interests, not only sexually but socially in all the dimensions of your life.

As a helper you may need to empower your helpees to realize that they can make choices and that to stand up for themselves at times demands great courage.

How to Be a Group Leader

One form of helping is to facilitate a group in which members work on solving mutual problems together, either through sharing or responding to a structured activity. Group therapy, support groups and groups organized around addiction recovery help many people. The ideal size for such groups is six to twelve people.

The two major components of these groups are content and process. Content is the reason the group is together, the subject matter being discussed, what group members say. Process is what happens to and between group members as the group unfolds. Some of the dynamics of group process are morals, atmosphere, participation, competition, conflict and cooperation.

A group leader or facilitator does not have an authoritarian role although he or she exercises authority by keeping the group at its task and by being aware of the process. An effective group leader initiates discussion, attempts to generate participation by all group members, helps the group to resolve conflict and protects the rights of each person there. Every group member has both the right to speak and the right to remain silent or to pass when questioned. While the group may challenge or criticize a group member, the leader also protects each member's right not to be psychologically demolished by the group.

A group leader also models what is appropriate in the group. If you expect your peers to be open and honest, then as a leader you need to demonstrate those qualities yourself. This openness in the group may be a gradual process as members learn to trust each other and become willing to take more risks. A group leader encourages members to respond to what the others have said, to identify with the experiences of the others and so realize that they are not alone in their problems. A group leader is responsible for helping the group to get started on time and to bring closure when it is time to end.

You may lead or co-lead a group activity for younger teens, for example, on a retreat day. You will have many responsibilities, even if you share the tasks with a co-facilitator. Be sure to participate in the group yourself while never dominating the conversation. You should not come across to the group as a detached disciplinarian in charge of the group. While you have the authority and responsibility to maintain order in the group and not allow horsing around, your main role is sensitively facilitating conversation and problem-solving. Many of the skills you have already learned for being an active listener will come into play in a group also. Here are "ten commandments" to help you in your role as a group leader.

Ten Commandments for a Group Leader

1. Remind the group of *confidentiality*. What is said in the group remains in the group. This is essential for building trust.

2. Have the group *sit close together*. Every group member should be able to see every other member. Don't let anyone sit outside of the group space.

3. *Make eye contact*. Fix your gaze on the person who is speaking. He or she may need the strength of your eyes to feel free to speak. Also be sure group members can all *see* each other easily.

4. *Don't give advice*—even when it is asked for. People need to solve their own problems. Don't fall into this easy trap because of your own need to be a helper. *Advice does not help, it hinders solutions.*

5. *Listen.* In any group, most of your time should be spent listening and using summarizing responses.

6. *Don't be afraid of silence.* The creativity and pressure of silence is far better than any pressure you may exert to get the group to speak.

7. *Sit on your own story* and your own problems. The group is not the place to go into *your* issues. You are there for others. If you wish to identify with the speaker, do so in a simple statement. (For example: "I kind of know what you mean because my father tends to yell too much too.") *Do not elaborate.*

8. *Watch for nonverbal clues.* Focus more on the feelings of the speakers than on their words. Words are often a protective screen for what is really going on inside. Observe how relaxed or nervous, hostile or depressed the person seems to be. For example, people who reveal supposedly heavy problems to the group in a perfectly relaxed manner are probably not being honest; people

whose eyes fill up when discussing something they say doesn't bother them are probably not being honest either.

9. *Keep the group discussion focused on one person's issues at a time.* Don't let one group member attract the attention of you or the group while another still has unfinished business. Never leave a person out there hanging. Ideally all group members should respond to each person's problem, but *at the very least*, the leader *must* respond.

10. *Touch.* If people become emotionally upset in the group they should be held, ideally by the people next to them in the group. If others don't respond, you as leader should move next to the person. It's also helpful to lay your hand on anyone in the group, especially a person who needs encouragement in speaking. You set the tone of the group. Your freedom in taking the risk to touch gives other group members permission to touch also.

Group Roles

Below is a list of roles that create dysfunctional behavior in the group. These negative roles challenge even a skillful leader.

Follower—Refrains from giving own point of view and allows rest of group to make decisions.

Clown—Spends most of the group time fooling around.

Blocker—Always disagrees with the group or else takes the group off track.

Shy—Doesn't contribute in the group.

Bored—Easily distracted during the group or withdraws from participation.

Dictator—Tries to control the group.

Talker—Monopolizes the group's time.

Peacemaker—Is uncomfortable with conflict or anger and tries to dismiss them.

Cynic—Challenges the task or process of the group.

Cross-examiner—Keeps focus on self by too many questions for others.

Intellectual—Can't or won't speak from a feeling level.

Red Crosser—Rushes to a defense of or alliance with a group member and prevents the group from continuing a conversation.

Projector—Puts feelings he or she has onto others; projects own viewpoints onto others.

Competer—Tops another's story or seeks leader's approval.

Sympathy Seeker—Exaggerates or dramatizes problems for attention and sympathy of the group.

Guidelines for Preparing a Talk

There are various types of talks. Let's review them quickly so that we can see how they vary:

Sermon—instruction in religion or morals, a serious talk on behavior, responsibility, etc.

Homily—a reflection on a passage from the Bible.

Instruction—knowledge, information given or taught.

Witness—testimony, a first-hand account of something.

Ordinarily, peer ministry talks should be a healthy balance of instruction and witness.

When giving a talk, first introduce yourself (where you're from, school, family, etc.). Keep in mind the following sentence as a guide to what your talk should be:

Say A Few Words.

Simple Statement—Define your topic.

Amplify—Share your knowledge on the subject.

Few Examples—Personal witness stories, testimony (one or two examples, depending on length and intensity). Be kind to other people who are not there to defend themselves. Own your emotions by using "I" instead of "you," especially if it is a point of critique. For example, say "I got angry!" rather than "You made me angry!"

Wrap it up—Pull things together, maybe offer a challenge. *Caution*: Don't get preachy! Don't tell people what they *have* to do. Invite them to look at themselves, their own experiences and see for themselves what needs to be done.

Below is an outline you might want to follow in preparing your talk.

A. Initial Thoughts

1. *Peer witness* is important. You have a lot of influence and power with one another. Use it positively. Young people will listen more readily to one another than to adults.

2. All of us have a *story*. Believe *you* have something to say. Trust your own experience. If you feel a certain way or have had a particular experience, be sure that others have felt the same way or have been through the same thing; they may find it helpful to know they are not alone.

3. Prepare well. Be in touch with how you feel at the moment of the talk. Be sincere and as natural as you can be. In other words *be yourself*.

B. Preparation

1. Find a *quiet spot*. Do what you need to do to slow down and put aside the day's distractions. You might listen to music or just sit and relax a while before you begin. Ask the Holy Spirit to inspire you, to help you prepare well for the benefit of those who hear you. Create a prayerful atmosphere and give yourself the time needed to do a good job.

2. Ask yourself: "What do *I* think, feel, believe about this topic?" For example, if the topic is Church, ask yourself: What does Church mean to me? What has been my felt experience of Church?

3. *Jot down* words, phrases, ideas that come to mind when you reflect on what the topic means to you. For example, if the topic is Church, you might jot down such things as "community, brothers and sisters, not just going to Mass."

4. Know and understand the *goal or purpose* of your talk. For example, if your topic is self-knowledge, the purpose of the talk might be to get across the importance of knowing yourself and the need to accept yourself.

5. Decide on the *main points* you want to make.

6. Organize an *outline* using these main points and any related points or ideas.

7. Use *personal examples*. For example, if your talk is on obstacles in relationships, think of a time when you've experienced a problem in a relationship due to fear or mistrust.

Additional helps in preparation

8. You may want to do some *background reading* on the topic. For example, if the topic is Jesus, it would be good to read and reflect on the gospel stories; if the topic is alcohol and drugs, it might be good to do some research on the causes of abuse.

9. You may want to begin or end your talk with a song that will reinforce the message or theme of the talk. This can create an atmosphere and set the tone of the talk. You could also use a favorite quote or reading.

Give Yourself Away

Remember that the ministry is the minister. Giving a talk should cost you something because you are truly giving a piece of yourself to your listeners. If you are superficial and evasive, no one will care what you say. If you are honest and speak from your heart, people will remember your talk for months, even years.

C. Delivery

1. Set the *mood*, create the atmosphere for your talk. You may want to play a song, offer a prayer or light a candle. Low lights can also help.

2. Be *comfortable* yourself. Decide whether it's best for you to sit or stand, whether you need a lectern or not. Take your time in order to be fully present to what you are doing and to become calm inside.

3. Make sure you have *eye contact* with everyone in the room. As you speak look at individuals.

4. In presenting your talk, take your time. *Don't rush*. Speak slowly and distinctly. It's best not to read your talk, but you should have an outline in front of you—at least key words. Be as natural as you can.

5. Afterward, no matter how you delivered your talk, *trust* that your words and your sincerity touched someone, perhaps in ways you may never know.

Ethical Standards and Confidentiality

As a person with a public identity within your church or school community, it is important to understand the ethics or code of behavior that apply to the helping dimension of peer ministry.

First, if you will clearly be using helping skills, it is essential that you receive the proper training for the tasks ahead. You also need to be clear about who supervises you. Who is the adult to whom you bring the situations in peer ministry that are beyond your ability to handle? This person should be clearly identified. If a team of adults is involved, you need to know if any team member is appropriate or if there is a designated individual.

The most important ethical issue for peer helpers is probably confidentiality. The National Peer Helpers Association has developed a national code of ethics and standards. First, in all of your dealings with fellow peer ministers and helpees where problems and personal issues are discussed, confidentiality is essential. It is extremely painful for a teenager who spoke of a personal matter on a retreat weekend, for example, to hear that matter discussed in school corridors on Monday. You have a serious obligation and responsibility to keep secret the personal confidences shared with you.

While we uphold confidentiality as a general principle, there are occasions when it is inappropriate and unethical to keep something secret. There are times when you need to refer a helpee's issues to your adult leader so that the proper intervention can occur, and so that you are protected from a legal and ethical standpoint. These exceptions are:

1. when a helpee threatens suicide;

2. when a helpee reports physical or sexual abuse;

3. when a helpee's life is in danger (for example, when anorexia or drug use has become life threatening);

4. when your or someone else's physical well-being has been threatened;

5. when a helpee exhibits psychotic behavior or some other form of mental illness;

6. any other situation that is beyond your own experience and expertise.

You have no option regarding these six categories. Referral is the route to go, either to your adult leader(s) *or* to the professionals or agencies designated for referral during this training. It isn't mean or cruel to break confidence in these situations, because they are way beyond your scope. The very fact that a peer has confided this matter to you is in itself a cry for help, even though he or she might attempt to swear you to secrecy. Beware of being trapped into confidentiality when a helpee tries to make you promise to keep secret a matter not yet disclosed. It's better to have a helpee or friend angry with you than for someone not to get needed help. It's better to lose a friendship than a friend.

    The best approach, at least for situations 1, 2 and 3, described earlier, is to say, "Because you and your well-being matter so much to me I just can't keep this a secret. If you won't go for help then I will have to seek it for you. This isn't something the two of us can solve." For you to keep this helpee's secret is to take on to yourself a responsibility far greater than you can bear. It is unfair to you and ultimately unfair to the helpee. Think of how you would feel if some tragedy later befell this individual and you were the only person who knew, who could have gotten help and didn't.

Reflection—Referral List

Take the time to find out about these resources in your local community:

Phone #

_____	nearest emergency room
_____	a shelter for runaways
_____	local department of youth services
_____	nearest rape crisis intervention center
_____	local Alcoholics Anonymous meeting
_____	local Alateen meeting
_____	local Narcotics Anonymous meeting
_____	suicide hotline
_____	AIDS hotline
_____	an adult I can talk with about helpees
_____	(other important numbers)

A Twenty-Four Hour Leadership Workshop

This overnight retreat experience focuses on leadership development and the identity of a ministering Christian. We usually think of leaders as those who rally the support of others, assertive and persuasive people who can influence others to follow them. Leadership in the context of peer ministry, though, follows Jesus' model of servant leadership. Christian leaders aren't afraid to look foolish, to stick to their own values no matter the cost, to serve the needy and downtrodden. Their own openness and authenticity challenge others to grow.

Journal Reflection #1

Complete these statements and then share your answers with your group.

1. A time somebody ministered to me when I really needed it...

2. A time I ministered to someone who really needed it...

Journal Reflection #2

Complete the following and then share your answers with your group.

1. A fear I have about being a peer minister is…

2. A risk I repeatedly find difficult to take is…

3. How do you feel about trusting Jesus to help you with your problems?

Part Four: Crisis Intervention

Fundamentals of Crisis Intervention

Crisis intervention, an essential part of peer ministry, is very different from active listening and the helping skills we've discussed in Part Three. Let's begin by defining a crisis as one very serious event or a string of events that together throw a person emotionally off balance. Methods this person ordinarily uses to cope with stress no longer work. When you encounter a crisis, you must act. Below are five steps for a helper to follow in the face of a crisis.

1. *Find out what happened.* You need to know what occurred, as best as the helpee can describe it. You may have to probe to get the helpee to tell you why he or she is in crisis if the reason isn't self-evident. Nearly always in a crisis, the helper functions as a "referral agency," getting the person to the help he or she needs. You have already filled out a list of resources in your community. This list can be important in the face of a crisis.

2. *Do the first thing that needs to be done.* Very often in a crisis some immediate action is needed: going to an emergency room, calling the police, stopping bleeding or washing a cut. Taking immediate action can help stabilize a crisis. Very often a person in a crisis has become a victim and loses the ability to take action. In such cases, it is crucial that the helper take charge.

3. *Keep calm.* When others are out of control, we cannot become emotionally upset as well. We further stabilize a crisis by keeping calm ourselves. This elicits trust and confidence from the helpee. We may have to suppress our own emotional reaction and wait to ventilate it later elsewhere.

4. *Encourage the helpee's coping skills.* Especially when victimization is involved and a sense of powerlessness results, it can be helpful to invite the helpee to start immediately to regain power by describing what has taken place. Another way to regain power is to make a decision—no matter how small—about what to do. For example, ask the helpee: Which hospital do you want to go to? Shall I take you to a friend's house? Do you want to call someone?

Reflection—Memory of a Crisis

Answer the following questions. You may want to share your answers with your group.

1. Have you ever been in a crisis, that is, in a state of mind in which your emotional balance was thrown off?

2. What stabilized the crisis for you in its early stages?

3. What do you recall as being most helpful to you during that time?

5. *Seek and use help*. Refer and/or take the helpee to the place that can provide the most help: the hospital, a rape counselor, a clergy person, a detox center, home, etc. In a crisis it is generally unwise to leave a person alone. Your local emergency room will have psychological as well as medical services or at least will be able to refer you to the agency that can provide the most help.

The major difference between crisis intervention and the listening skills you have learned is that often in a crisis you need to break confidentiality and get outside help. Young people coping with the issues discussed in these sections usually need not only peer support but also professional assistance that you cannot provide. Recall from our discussion of ethical standards that you are *required* to break confidentiality when someone is a threat to you, themselves or others, or any time their problems are beyond your own experience or expertise. You need to get help for the person. First of all they need a level of intervention that you cannot provide; secondly you need to protect yourself. As a peer minister in a formal, structured program, you have a definite role. If you are later judged to have provided insufficient or incorrect help to a peer in crisis while acting in that role, you could be held legally liable or responsible.

Go to your adult leader(s) when you receive information beyond your expertise. Remember that peer ministry is not only acquiring skills to be a more effective helper; it also involves the humility to acknowledge the limits of your own experience and competence. Peer ministry takes place in the context of a Christian community where we can turn to others for professional expertise that we don't possess or to caring adults whose life experience has given them the wisdom to respond to critical issues appropriately.

Alcohol and Other Drugs

The most prevalent "recreational" drug in the United States is alcohol. According to some estimates, there are at least three million teenage alcoholics, and twenty-five percent of all teenagers live in alcoholic families. If your parent is an alcoholic, you are more likely than the general population to have an alcoholic problem; there appears to be a genetic disposition toward alcoholism. Alcoholism is a progressive disease. It can never be cured, only treated. Alcoholics who have stopped drinking (and perhaps also attend Alcoholics Anonymous meetings) talk about themselves as recover*ing*, not recovered.

Alcoholism and other forms of drug addiction are especially dangerous for teenagers. Peer pressure is especially powerful when a person is still in the process of shaping an identity. Also adolescents seem to develop addictions more quickly than adults in our society. Alcoholism is life-threatening. If a helpee confides this problem to you, you need to seek help and intervention. But such a revelation is rare since most alcoholics deny that they have a problem. Sometimes this denial is expressed in statements like "I only drink beer"; "I never drink alone"; "I only drink on weekends"; "I could quit at any time." Statements like these are simply excuses and rationalizations; skilled helpers need to perceive them as such. For example, let's address the myth that beer is not problematic. Six beers are equivalent to three mixed drinks. They produce 0.09% concentration of alcohol in the blood (for an "average" person of about 150 pounds). It takes six hours for the alcohol to leave the body. The alcohol causes exaggerated emotions and behavior.

A person has a problem with alcohol if it has a negative effect on at least one part of his or her life: family, friendships, job, economics, spirituality. Alcoholics usually begin by drinking socially; they begin to look forward to the next drinking opportunity (for example, a keg party next weekend). That anticipation can lead them to getting drunk with regularity and even experiencing blackouts (alcohol-induced amnesia). Alcoholics begin drinking more than they intend and making excuses for their drinking. When the drinking becomes compulsive, then alcoholism has set in.

It used to be thought that alcoholics had to "hit bottom," that is, to experience severe negative consequences of their drinking, before they would let go of denial and admit to having a problem. While hitting bottom may still be necessary for some people, it is far better if intervention can occur at an earlier stage, before drinking progresses to alcoholism.

If a friend or helpee has a problem with alcohol or even is only at the stage of regular use (which leads to higher tolerance), don't lecture, threaten or argue. Recognize the denial, but encourage the person to seek treatment. Let him know that you can only support him if his behavior changes. If he's reluctant to go to an A.A. meeting alone, find a meeting that is open and offer to go along.

Ted only drank on weekends, but it was every weekend in the year. His friends began to notice that once he had a couple of beers he continued "pounding" them down. He didn't seem able to stop until he was totally drunk. When his buddies eventually confronted Ted and told him he had a drinking problem, he denied it to them and also to himself. Gradually he moved toward a new set of friends and drinking partners. His old friends continued to hound him and confront him with his behavior. Finally, almost a year later, Ted agreed to go to an A.A. meeting after a binge of almost a week of drinking. He was no longer able to confine it to weekends. The constant confrontation of *real* friends finally got Ted to face his denial. Without that loving confrontation, who knows where Ted would be today?

A few years back, I knew a student named Mark who was having a difficult time in high school and needed to talk to someone about it. He appeared to be a normal teenager, yet he knew he was depressed. He was involved in school sports and had many friends. He talked about being bored with his routine of going to school all week and just partying on the weekends. He couldn't remember how he began drinking and smoking pot and didn't see himself as a person with "a problem." He used to say to me, "I don't want you to think I'm a druggie or anything. I just do it because there's nothing else to do, and sometimes it's kind of fun."

Mark was into a routine shared by many teenagers. He had never considered not partying in this way. One week he came in and talked about being tired of the same old thing. He said he wanted to do something different on the weekends. He was afraid he wouldn't be able to find any friends to do something other than drinking. He explained that he felt most of the people he hung out with really didn't know him for the person he was. When I asked him what he could do to change any of these situations, he said he could just stop going out with his group of party friends, but he was still concerned that he'd have nothing else to do. Another option he came up with was to continue being with his friends but just stop partying with them. He was afraid they would look down on him or would feel he thought he was better than them. He wasn't sure he had the strength to do this. He said he would try not drinking or smoking when they went out that weekend.

He came in the following week to tell me that he tried to abstain on Friday night, but his friends thought he was joking when he refused a joint being passed around. "I was trying," he said, "and I made it through most of the night, but I did end up smoking a few hits. I felt like a jerk for not smoking, and then I felt like a jerk after I got high." He was confused, but at least he had considered it. He told me of a kid at the party who didn't have a beer in his hand or get

Reflection—Self Inventory

Answer these questions honestly, "yes" or "no."

1. Have you ever made excuses for your drinking? _____

2. Do you drink so you will feel less shy with others? _____

3. Do you dislike a party where there is no alcohol? _____

4. Do you ever miss school or work because of drinking? _____

5. Do you ever drink alone? _____

6. Do most of your friends also drink? _____

7. Have you ever had a blackout or loss of memory due to drinking? _____

8. When you drink do you find it hard to stop? _____

9. Do you have to drink to go out on a date? _____

10. Do you react defensively when others try to discuss your drinking with you? _____

11. Do you ever drink to build up your self-confidence? _____

12. Do you ever try to hide your drinking from others? _____

13. Do you drink to escape worries at home or elsewhere? _____

14. Do you find you have to drink more now to get a good feeling? _____

15. Have you ever driven while drunk? _____

If you answered "yes" to any one question, this is a warning or red flag. Think about how alcohol is affecting your life. If you answered "yes" to several questions, then it is time to talk with someone about your drinking.

high all night. "Everyone was talking to him," he said. The following week Mark didn't do any drugs. He said he went out with his friends and still had a pretty good time. People asked him what was wrong with him, and he replied, "I'm not into it." He was shocked that no one really gave him a hard time. As time went on he felt more comfortable being in situations where drugs were around, but not getting involved with them. He was convinced that more people talked to him at parties than they ever did while he was doing what everyone else was doing. He also began to do better in school. He said he had more confidence in himself and he felt more mature.

I share this with you to show you how young people can take a stand about what they want to do and maintain their own value system. All of Mark's fears about how others would perceive him were worse than how others actually saw him. I'm sure Mark felt better about himself when he learned others would accept him for what he chose to do. This drastically reduced the stress that had become so much a part of his daily life.

Some Other Drugs

While alcohol is the most used and abused drug in this country, others have serious consequences as well.

Marijuana (Cannabis Sativa). This drug may be smoked or taken orally (for example, in food). Its chronic use can lead to distortion of memory and puts the person at higher risk for cancer, emphysema and bronchitis. It is estimated that marijuana smoke contains fifty percent more cancer-causing materials than tobacco smoke. A psychological dependency on this drug can develop.

Cocaine. This drug may be snorted, taken orally, smoked or injected. Its chronic use can lead to restlessness, irritability, psychosis and depression. It is expensive and extremely addicting, especially psychologically.

Crack cocaine. "Crack" is the street name given to cocaine that has been converted to a smokable base. It takes effect rapidly and the short-lived high may be followed by irritability or severe depression. The enormous craving for another high can cause psychological addiction within a few days.

Heroin. This drug may be snorted or injected into the veins. Tolerance and physical dependence develop very quickly. Withdrawal symptoms are severe. Death from overdose is not uncommon.

Mescaline. This drug is smoked or swallowed as capsules or tablets. Similar to LSD, its chronic use can lead to delusions, panic and psychosis. It is a hallucinogenic drug (like LSD, PCP and "mushrooms") and can produce flashbacks.

Amphetamines. These drugs, often called "speed" or "uppers," can be taken orally or injected. Chronic use can cause irritability and psychosis. Psychological dependence develops quickly.

Barbiturates. These drugs can be taken orally, intravenously or rectally. Used in combination with alcohol, barbiturates can be lethal. Chronic use can result in brain and liver damage, confusion and withdrawal. Both physical and psychological dependence can develop.

Nicotine. This drug is smoked and acts as a stimulant to the central nervous system. Chronic use can lead to cancers of the throat, lungs, mouth and esophagus as well as heart disease and emphysema. Cigarette smoking especially leads to a strong physical and psychological dependency.

Drug of Choice

When people have developed an addiction to alcohol, marijuana, cocaine or another drug, there is often a preferred substance or "drug of choice." But it's also important to realize that in today's society most addicts use more than one drug, either to intensify the sensation of the substance or to counteract its effects: e.g., a person who uses cocaine might also use marijuana to "bring him down" if he's too wired.

Pregnancy, Abortion and Sexual Activity

As a young Christian you already know the Church's stance that sex should be reserved to marriage. This viewpoint isn't intended to be an attack on pleasure, but rather a preservation of deeper happiness. When people aren't ready for an emotional commitment to each other within the stability of marriage, sexual activity will ultimately cause pain when the relationship ends. Abstinence protects young people in today's society from sexually transmitted diseases like herpes, syphilis, gonorrhea and HIV/AIDS. Abstinence also protects against pregnancy; only marriage offers an infant the best advantage for a stable relationship.

Yet we know that many young Christians are sexually active despite the wisdom of the Church. Like all of the gospel ideals, the appropriate expression of our sexuality is a challenge, an ideal for which we strive. We sometimes fall short due to human weakness. In fact the Greek verb for *sin* means to miss the bull's eye. In other words, sin is falling short of the ideal.

The Troubled Journey is the report of a study prepared by Search Institute for the Lutheran Brotherhood and published in 1990. (*The Troubled Journey: A Portrait of 6th-12th Grade Youth*, is available from the Lutheran Brotherhood, 625 Fourth Ave. South, Minneapolis, MN 55415.) The study involved fifty thousand young people in grades six to twelve in over one hundred public schools. It gives us insight into the sexual behavior of teens today and the reasons beneath the behavior. A major point in this study is the connection between sexual activity and "at risk" behaviors.

Here is a list of ten "deficits." The more of these deficits a young person has, the more likely he or she is to be sexually active. The deficits are (1) alone at home a lot; (2) selfish values; (3) overexposure to TV; (4) attends drinking parties; (5) has real stress; (6) is a victim of physical abuse; (7) reports sexual abuse; (8) one or both parents have addictions; (9) is isolated socially; (10) is affected by negative peer pressure.

You may know peers who are sexually active and for whom none of these deficits apply. But keep in mind that in many cases they do. In other words, when dealing with a helpee's sexual behavior you may be dealing with many other factors as well. Conversely the same study reports that young people who follow their church's guidelines about abstinence (1) have been taught to appreciate abstinence as a value, (2) are involved in their church and (3) are motivated to do well in school.

Self-esteem is a major factor in sexual activity and teen pregnancy. If a young person feels unloved or has low self-esteem, he or she may attempt to fill that gap with sexual activity. But the sex does little to change self-concept. In fact it often leads to guilt or shame which adds to deterioration of self-worth. Alcohol is another factor. Often teenage sex occurs when good judgment has been blurred by the use of alcohol.

Pregnancy

Teenage pregnancy is at an epidemic level in this country, the highest rate of any other developed nation despite the prevalence of birth control. *The Troubled Journey* reports that about half of teenagers do not use birth control when engaging in sex, which of course increases the chance of a pregnancy.

Why do so many young women seem to choose to get pregnant? Again it relates to self-esteem. If a girl has a poor self-image, she may have sex with a boy to please him, to win his acceptance (which is often mistaken for love). If she thinks no one loves her, she may think that if she has a child, then at last somebody will love her. She is probably not even consciously aware of these motives.

If you are trying to help a sexually active peer, realize that it isn't just strong sexual desire that is operative. A lot is going on inside this person and in the factors that make up her life-style and network of relationships.

Abortion

The Christian Churches are opposed to abortion. Yet for teenagers who have made the mistake of being sexually active, sometimes abortion seems like a quick fix to an immediate problem and embarrassment. If you have been approached by a friend to discuss the possibility of abortion, you can refer her to one of several fine agencies, where people will discuss the matter from a Christian perspective. If she will not seek help, here are a few factual objections you can offer. While not judging her you can state your personal feelings about an abortion.

1. Teenagers who have abortions are more at risk for suicide attempts after the abortion.

2. Teenagers are more likely to have severe nightmares after an abortion.

3. Many teenagers report a worsened self-esteem after an abortion.

4. Women who report being rushed into a decision about an abortion report the greatest severity of psychological problems following an abortion.

5. While an adolescent may see herself simply as someone who has "had an abortion," she may later see herself as someone who has "destroyed a child."

6. A teenager who has an abortion may experience an inability to grow and mature normally.

These six dangers apply solely to teenagers (from *Association for Interdisciplinary Research Newsletter*, Vol. 3, No. 3, Fall 1990, Association for Interdisciplinary Research Values and Social Change, 419 7th Street NW, Suite 500, Washington D.C. 20004). More research is available that tells how abortion can impact a woman physically and also how future marriage and childbearing can be affected.

Abuse

There are three kinds of abuse: emotional, physical and sexual. Very often these are combined. Let's look at physical abuse first. This is the most obvious, the easiest to detect. A child or teenager who is abused learns to cope through survival mechanisms such as: (a) being passive to avoid being hurt anymore; (b) being aggressive and full of rage; (c) not being developmentally equal to peers (energy is used to protect themselves).

People who misuse power or who do not know how to resolve conflict through communication resort to abusive actions. Out of embarrassment many victims deny the abuse and attribute obvious injuries to other causes. As a helper be aware that denial of abuse is common. If you suspect a helpee is presently being physically abused, discuss this with your adult leader who can initiate plans for intervention. Remember to try not to appear shocked when abuse is confided to you. Do not be judgmental about the abuse. Victims often harbor very ambivalent feelings toward those who abuse them and sometimes even feel that they deserve to be hurt. No one, no matter what the shortcomings, deserves to be abused. Such behavior should never be tolerated for any reason.

Sexual abuse is far more common than it may appear. A 1980 survey in California and Massachusetts found that one in five girls and one in seven boys under the age of eighteen had been sexually abused. Socially, while it is still difficult for young women to admit to being abused, it is even more difficult for young men since it raises the additional issue of homosexuality if the perpetrator was male. More recent studies suggest that the rate of sexual abuse of both boys and girls has risen during the past fourteen years. Sexual abuse usually occurs between people who know each other well. In fact, because there is trust in the relationship the abuser was able to take advantage of the younger person. Abuse often occurs gradually, beginning with fondling or touching and perhaps moving to penetration. Abusers are people with psychological problems who attempt to work out their frustration or intimacy needs in a sexual way. They often don't perceive their actions as wrong. Victims are becoming more open about their experiences (part of the healing process), but males are still less open than females.

Some Signs of Abuse

Physical
- bruises
- burns
- lacerations and abrasions
- skeletal injuries
- head injuries
- internal injuries from blows to the abdomen

Sexual
- bruises or bleeding in the genital or anal areas
- venereal disease
- pregnancy
- unusual sexual knowledge
- delinquency
- runaway behavior

Emotional
- excessive shyness
- self-defeating behavior
- deep feelings of inadequacy
- misdirected anger or rage

How to Help a Victim

1. Believe the story of abuse. These aren't the kinds of revelations that people generally enjoy making up.

2. Be clear that abuse is never the victim's fault, even if he or she cares for the abuser, enjoys the relationship otherwise or experienced sexual pleasure when abused.

3. Validate the victim's feelings of anger, pain, fear, etc.

4. If the abuse is in the past and the victim is out of danger, encourage professional counseling or a support group of other victims so that the healing process can begin.

5. If the abuse is present and ongoing, refer the matter to your adult supervisor so that the necessary intervention can occur. Trust that the information confided to you is indeed a cry for help.

Emotional abuse is difficult to prove legally, but it is widespread. It occurs when a person is continually "put down" by a parent or family member so that feelings of self-worth deteriorate and the individual becomes insecure and lacks confidence.

Rape

"Aggravated rape" is done by a stranger using a weapon. Far more common is "date rape" or "acquaintance rape" involving friends or former boyfriends. Exploitive sexual relationships most commonly involve a male abusing a female, but can also involve a female abusing a male or another female, or a male abusing a male. In "acquaintance rape" verbal pressure followed by grabbing and shoving often replaces more obvious violence. This type of exploitation crosses all social classes and races.

As a helper, don't underestimate the possible negative effects of forced sexual contact with someone known. Many victims confuse their own submission with consent; this generates feelings of guilt, confusion, wanting to isolate themselves, difficulty in trusting and inability to concentrate in school. Sometimes reactions are even more extreme. Feelings may lead to behavior like running away, drug abuse, prostitution or even suicide.

What is the profile of the person who commits sexual assault? The adult rapist often has not learned to deal with his own anger and seeks dominance and power over another person. The teenager who assaults others sexually tends to be a victim of abuse from a family with communication problems and where affection isn't displayed. He may also be under pressure to be an achiever. People who have been sexually or physically abused themselves are more likely to commit a sexual assault on others. Most rapists are young men between the ages of fifteen and twenty-four.

Most rape victims are young women between the ages of fifteen and nineteen. No one ever *deserves* to be raped no matter what situation she puts herself in or how she dresses. Consent is a choice made when people have equal power. Giving in out of fear is not consent. Even going along with something because of fear of how your behavior might seem to a group is not consent.

How to Respond to a Rape Victim

1. Do not blame or judge the victim.

2. Realize that she or he has been violated by a terrifying experience and feels overwhelmed by powerlessness and loss of control.

3. If medical attention is required, get it immediately.

4. Take or refer the victim to experts in the field of rape intervention, for example, a local hotline or agency that deals with rape victims.

5. Discuss the matter with your adult supervisor.

Eating Disorders

Eating disorders are a serious problem among young people today. It is estimated that twelve percent of girls ages thirteen to eighteen are affected. Boys are also susceptible to eating disorders, for example, as a result of the pressure to lose weight for wrestling competitions. An eating disorder is a way to cope with stress and anxiety. When people feel a lack of control in their lives, eating is one area that they can control. There are two kinds of eating disorders: anorexia nervosa and bulimia.

Anorexic people have a distorted sense of being overweight. The contemporary notion of the ideal female figure holds up an image of beauty that many cannot achieve. People with anorexia refuse to eat and sometimes this refusal leads to starvation and even death. As the disease progresses it becomes more observable even though the victim may be in denial. Anorexia is life-threatening; it calls for intervention.

Bulimia, which sometimes alternates with anorexia, consists of "binge and purge" behaviors. Compulsive overeating is followed by enemas, laxatives or self-induced vomiting. These behaviors are accompanied by feelings of guilt and shame. Bulimia often remains hidden for a long period of time. While not as life-threatening as anorexia, it too requires intervention to stop the self-destructive cycle. This disease is often brought about by a life change that causes stress and anxiety, for example, moving away from home to college.

Obesity is not technically considered a disorder, although it is a serious problem. "Overeaters Anonymous" (O.A.) is an excellent support group for people who eat compulsively out of depression or some other emotion. It is built upon the twelve steps of Alcoholics Anonymous.

The following characteristics may appear in young people with an eating disorder:

1. They feel life's circumstances are beyond their control.

2. They tend to be achievers, perfectionists, always attempting to satisfy the expectations others have of them.

3. They use alcohol and/or some other drug or they come from homes where substance abuse exists.

Urge your helpee to get both medical and psychological attention. If he or she will not do this voluntarily, discuss an intervention plan with your adult leader.

> **Identifying the Victim of Bulimia**
>
> 1. Excessive concern with weight gain and body image
> 2. Periods of strict dieting followed by eating binges
> 3. Frequent overeating especially when distressed
> 4. Planning binges or opportunities to binge
> 5. Binging on high calorie, easily ingested and often sweet food
> 6. Feeling out of control in regard to eating patterns
> 7. Guilt or shame following binge-purge episodes
> 8. Secretiveness about binges and purges
> 9. Awareness that the eating pattern is abnormal
> 10. Disappearing after a meal for the purpose of purging
> 11. Self-deprecating thoughts and feelings of hopelessness and depression
> 12. Resistance to seeking professional help and sabotaging treatment
>
> Muus, Rolf E., "Adolescent Eating Disorder Bulimia," *Adolescence*, Vol. 21, #82, Summer, 1986.

Divorce and Blended Families

While divorce is commonplace today, it is still one of the most difficult issues for a teenager to handle. Just when young people begin to figure out who they are and to gain a sense of identity, the ground beneath them shifts, their whole world topples over. Even when parents try to protect their children from their own bitterness or pain, divorce is difficult to handle. Teens whose parents are divorcing may still feel "different" from peers. Their family is a "failure" when measured against the "successful" families of friends. This is often accompanied by self-doubt and questions like: "Was it my fault?," "Could I have kept them together somehow?" Even when parents tell their children that the separation has nothing to do with them, these irrational questions can linger. Despite their efforts to the contrary, parents will often seek support and allegiance from their teenage children for their own reasons for the divorce. This can create a lot of tension for children torn between two parents.

The experience of being in a family of divorce can cause a wide range of difficult feelings for a young person. As a helper or friend you can be a support by being a good listener. Remember that the real issue isn't so much the events but the feelings that these events trigger. Focus on your helpee's *feelings*. It might be helpful for your helpee to join a local support group for teenagers who are going through a divorce and/or adjusting to being members of a blended family.

Sue had a rocky period during her teenage years. Her parents divorced and Sue stayed with her mother in their home. Her father moved to a condo in the same city. Within a year Sue's mother had a boyfriend and her father was engaged to be married to a new partner. Sue was tossed between the bitterness of both parents and seemed confused about who deserved her loyalty. She also had to deal with strangers moving into her parents' lives. Sue became irritable with her friends. Her grades started to decline and she started to party more regularly. Her moods swung from intense anger to not caring about anything at all.

A peer minister in school eventually convinced Sue to join a support group for "teenagers of divorce." While the group couldn't do anything about the actions of Sue's parents, it did give her a place to ventilate her feelings: sadness, anger, resentment, confusion. She quickly

---

Feelings a Child of Divorce May Experience

Anger—at parents for "ruining" the family

Abandonment—feeling that a parent has "left" you

Guilt—about being angry at your parents when you know they are also having a rough time *or* about being a contributing cause for the divorce, that somehow you are to blame

Fear—of being "caught in the middle"

Sadness—that the family entity you knew has "died"

Betrayal—feeling that your parents deceived you

Embarrassment—taking on your parents' failure as your own

Worry—about financial security

Resentful—about having to deal with this problem when you already have enough to deal with

Relief—that conflict in the house will cease

realized that she was not alone, that many kids were dealing with similar issues. The remainder of her high school years were still a struggle, but now that she is in college and living away from home, Sue says that the support group she was in and the friends she made there kept her from falling into self-destructive behaviors during that vulnerable period of her life.

It is crucial that teenagers talk out these feelings. If suppressed, the feelings will be a continual source of anxiety. Some may attempt to escape the feelings by partying, delinquency, sexual activity or extreme busyness. None of these are healthy alternatives. A good listener can make a world of difference for a young person in pain from an impending or present divorce.

Children's Bill of Rights in Divorce Actions

1. **The right to a continuing relationship with both parents.**
2. **The right to be treated as an important human being with unique feelings, ideas and desires.**
3. **The right to continuing care and guidance from both parents.**
4. **The right to know and appreciate what is good in each parent without one parent degrading the other.**
5. **The right to express love, affection and respect for each parent without having to stifle that love because of fear of disapproval by the other parent.**
6. **The right to know that the parents' decision to divorce was not the responsibility of the child.**
7. **The right not to be a source of argument between the parents.**
8. **The right to honest answers to questions about the changing family relationships.**
9. **The right to be able to experience regular and consistent contact with both parents and to know the reason for cancellation of time or change of plans.**
10. **The right to have a relaxed, secure relationship with both parents without being placed in a position to manipulate one parent against the other.**

Source: Dane County Family Court Counseling service, Madison, Wis.

Stepfamilies or 'Blended Families'

It's estimated that almost fifty percent of marriages will end in divorce. Most divorced people remarry and many of them have children. Some stepfamilies or blended families are due to the death of one parent. All blended families are formed out of personal loss. This is a crucial difference from the biological family. Children have "lost" a parent through death or divorce and at least one of the parents (if not both) has lost a partner. People in the family will be grieving this loss at various paces and in different ways. This phenomenon makes it difficult to achieve a *happy* blended family initially. Also, children usually have no choice about belonging to this new family, which has its own set of problems.

Other possible problem areas in blended families include:

- New and old traditions/ways of doing things in and as a family
- Who disciplines whom, how and for what reasons
- Custody and visitation rights of other parent(s)
- Relating to new siblings
- Unrealistic parental expectations for speedy harmony within the family
- Living in a new house/community; being in a new school

As a helper you first need to realize that if your helpee is adjusting to a new family system, this is a long and complex process. As a matter of fact, some teenagers choose not to adjust, since they will be out of the house soon. You can be a good listener to inner struggles and mixed feelings. You might be able to encourage your helpee to work at being a member of this family, to view it as an opportunity for new growth. You might only be able to be a sounding board. That's OK. Your role as a helper is never to *solve* the stress that others experience.

Death and Loss

When people lose a friend, a family member, a classmate or a coworker, they enter a period of crisis. Often unknowingly they begin the complicated process known as grieving. Dr. Elisabeth Kübler-Ross, the widely known psychiatrist, describes the grief process in her book *On Death and Dying*. Through her interviews with the terminally ill, she was able to capture their thoughts, attitudes, needs and feelings about their own deaths. While she focused on the patients themselves, the five stages she has developed also are commonly experienced by the person who has suffered the death of a loved one.

The first of these five stages is *denial*. This stage refers to the shock of losing someone we love. We struggle to believe that our family member or friend has died. We may hope that tomorrow we will awake and discover that the news was a dream.

The second stage is *anger*. Once we realize that death has taken the person, we may be angry. Perhaps we will be angry at the person for leaving us alone before we could say good-bye. Anger toward ourselves and even anger at the whole world is common. We should allow ourselves to be angry for it may help us to deal with the sadness and pain beneath our anger.

The third stage is *bargaining*. Many people will try to bargain with God to bring the loved one back, saying something like, "I'll do anything you want, just please let me have some more time with my friend."

The fourth stage, *depression*, is often the hardest stage to get through and can last a long time. Realizing the permanency of what has happened usually makes hope for present or future happiness seem dim. Many things will be different. Much has changed. Depression can linger for months or years. Each person will encounter a different level and type of depression.

Acceptance, the final stage, is highlighted by a person's willingness to "let go" and attempt to go on with life. A dying person may accept death more easily than those who are left behind. For survivors, acceptance may come only after a long and difficult struggle.

Remember that these five stages are not cut in stone. A dying person or a person grieving another's death may not experience all of these stages. Also, these stages rarely occur in neat order. We may sink immediately into depression and then surface angry or in denial. Initially we may seem to accept death's reality and later find ourselves bargaining with God to bring someone back. Whether we are present while someone is dying or comforting someone grieving over a loss of another, we must be patient.

It may be hard to be around someone who is grieving, but we should not try to ease our awkwardness by pushing someone to go on who is not ready. We may encounter someone who has been depressed or angry over a death for a few years. The best thing we can do is help the person talk about it and try to work through it. We can reassure a grieving friend or helpee by offering a listening ear. We can't take away the heartache of a loss, but we can let others know that they are not alone in their pain.

Reflection

If you are going to be with others in their grief and sense of loss, it's important to face your own mortality and fears surrounding death.

Answer the following questions and share your answers with your group.

1. Have you ever experienced the death of someone close to you? If not, have you ever experienced the death of a beloved pet?

2. Can you relate to Dr. Kübler-Ross' five stages in any way?

3. Do you have any fears about death?

4. Does your Christian faith offer you any comfort when you think about death?

5. What helped you most when you were grieving?

What a Helper Can Do for a Grieving Friend

1. *Be there.* Your physical presence is more of a comfort than any words you might speak. Don't worry about the inadequacy of your words.

2. *Allow feelings* to be expressed. Let your friend or helpee verbalize whatever is going on inside.

3. *Attend the funeral service*, go to the funeral parlor or participate in whatever rituals the family enters into to commemorate the deceased. Your presence is a support.

4. *Don't attempt to cheer up your friend.* Let her feel what she feels. Don't preach to her. Even Christian belief in the Resurrection may not be comforting due to the overwhelming feelings of grief. That's OK. You will sense the right time to share your faith.

5. *Don't neglect your friend* after the period of bereavement. When the funeral is over and friends and family go away, a grieving person is often neglected at the very time when the pain is most acute. Continue to be there and don't set any time limit on the grieving period. Don't decide when your friend should be "over it" and "get on with life." The grieving period is personal and varies with each person.

Reflection

Write briefly about a loss you have experienced that didn't involve actual death. Share this experience with your group.

Other Losses: 'Little Deaths'

Death is not the only loss. All through our lives we will be with each other through many types of loss. When a relationship breaks up, when a parent leaves, when a friend moves away, when we graduate from high school, all of these (and many more) are forms of death and loss. Many of the same dynamics applicable to physical death and the grieving process occur in these experiences. You can be a good friend or helper in many of the same ways.

HIV Infection/ AIDS

The most dreaded infection in the world today is called HIV, Human Immunodeficiency Virus, which breaks down the immune system and renders it vulnerable to a variety of life-threatening infections. This condition is called AIDS (Acquired Immune Deficiency Syndrome). Having the HIV infection is not the same as having AIDS. HIV lasts for varying time periods, sometimes years, when a person experiences various symptoms such as chronic fatigue, swollen glands, loss of appetite, headaches, diarrhea, etc. Not all people experience the same symptoms.

HIV is a fragile virus that cannot be caught from the air or in water, or from objects and surfaces. It is transmitted by semen, blood and blood products, and vaginal and cervical secretions. It is transmitted most effectively by anal and vaginal intercourse or by sharing a needle (e.g., for tattooing, ear piercing or shooting drugs like anabolic steroids). While an intact latex condom, when properly used, reduces the risk of transmitting HIV, it doesn't remove the risk entirely. So many teenagers who have sex do not use condoms, and those that do may not use them properly.

The Christian value of abstinence from sexual intercourse before marriage not only makes moral sense; it also makes common sense in today's world. The HIV infection can remain dormant within a person's body for quite some time; he or she may be completely unaware that it is being transmitted to a sexual partner.

Below are some suggestions for being a helper to a friend or peer with HIV infection or AIDS.

1. If the person has engaged in a risky behavior, encourage testing for the virus. All major cities and many towns have anonymous "alternate" test sites where a person can go with complete confidence. These sites also provide pre-test and post-test counseling. If people get treatment soon rather than later, their chances of survival increase.

2. Stand by the person in the early stages of diagnosis. He or she will probably be on a roller-coaster of feelings from denial to hopelessness, to hope, to wanting to learn about the illness, to shame and guilt for having contracted the virus.

3. Don't judge the person. Let go of your curiosity about how the person became infected. He or she may not know, and more importantly it really doesn't matter. If he wants to tell you at some point how he thinks he became infected, listen, but there is no reason to probe.

4. Be with your helpee as others react to him. Sometimes out of fear, ignorance or moral self-righteousness the person's friends and even family members turn away from a person who is HIV positive. Others may treat the infected person differently. The individual may need to develop a new support network.

5. Encourage both proper medical treatment and psychological support. Support groups for people living with HIV and AIDS help them feel less isolated and more hopeful in their struggles.

6. A positive diagnosis can precipitate guilt and re-examination of one's life. Be a nonjudgmental listener and encourage any positive changes the person may choose to make.

7. Take care of yourself emotionally. If you remain close to your friend or helpee for the duration of the illness, you will experience many emotions. You will probably become more aware of your own mortality and if this individual is (or becomes) close to you, you will need to deal with your own grief issues as his health deteriorates. You will need a listening ear to allow you to unburden your own feelings in this situation. Many communities today also have support groups for the caregivers and loved ones of people living with HIV and AIDS.

Runaways

On any given night there are between three thousand and ten thousand homeless teenagers in New York City alone, according to the Legal Action Center for the homeless. Homeless teens fall into two categories:

(a) *lockouts and throwaways*. These young people are locked out of their homes by parents or guardians. Some of them use drugs, have left school or behave in ways their parents cannot tolerate. Sometimes it's an economic decision. Fifty percent of the homeless youth population is in this category.

(b) *runaways*. These teenagers leave home because of situations they cannot tolerate (like abuse, neglect and family conflicts).

As a helper, how do you respond to a helpee who tells you she wants to run away from home? The first step is to *assess* the situation. If this person is being abused sexually or physically, then she should leave home, at least for a while. Agencies in your local community can assist abuse victims. Such young people need temporary shelter. The state department of social services should be contacted so that parents will know what has occurred, so that the child will be safe and so that the proper intervention will occur.

After you assess the situation you may sense that if communication were better in this home this individual would not run away. In this case you would want to encourage your helpee to initiate communication with his parents (or whomever is the source of tension). If that seems impossible encourage him to seek professional counseling so that at least he will have an appropriate and helpful place to ventilate feelings.

Sometimes family members need a little space from each other. A helpee or friend may turn to you after a major unresolved argument with a parent. It might be healthy for the family if your friend spent a couple of nights at someone else's house to "cool off." If this is the case, encourage him to notify his parents of his whereabouts or seek their permission to stay elsewhere. Some teenagers punish their parents by causing them extreme worry about their whereabouts. This isn't really fair, and it doesn't help to heal the source of the conflict.

The streets are a dangerous place for a homeless teenager and are never a wise alternative to any problem. Your helpee may need a dose of reality. Warn him about the danger of being adrift. Kids on the street do not generally have the education or skills to find a good job. No one wants to hire a person without an address. Some get by on public assistance and others turn to prostitution to make money. Drugs are a big part of the street culture and it's easy to pick up a habit when you're depressed and down and out. AIDS, sexually transmitted diseases, fights and violent deaths are part and parcel of living on the streets in any urban area of this country.

No matter how dysfunctional a home is, it provides a sense of belonging. Even when abuse exists, a social worker's first goal will be to try to stop the abuse so that the young person can go back where she "belongs." Teenagers, like people of every age, need to learn that running away usually only adds more problems to a person's life. Learning how to communicate (including arguing) is the only way for families to be together in this stress-filled society of ours.

Suicide

Suicide is the second leading cause of death among teenagers today in the United States. Feeling isolated, helpless and without hope, suicidal people assume there is no solution to their problems. Such feelings can arise from family conflicts, the death of a friend or family member, divorce, the end of a romance, failure to gain a spot on a team or in a play, or the usual pressure to achieve and succeed in life.

It is common for people to think about suicide at some point in their lives. If you hear someone make a threat or even speak of suicide, take it seriously. Almost everyone who attempts suicide has given some clues beforehand. Statements like "They'll be sorry when I'm dead" or "Life isn't worth living anymore" are serious words not to be taken lightly.

If you suspect that a friend is suicidal, the best thing to do is ask. If the answer is yes, try not to appear overly anxious. The next thing to ask is "How do you plan to do it?" The response you get may scare you, and the more detailed the plan, the higher the likelihood that the person will take action. Don't be drawn into a promise not to tell anyone. Try to be honest and let the troubled person know you are going to get help. What may seem like an act of betrayal could save your friend's life. Most people in this situation don't really want to die, but they see no other way to escape the pain. They find a permanent solution to a temporary problem.

Profile of the Suicidal Person?

There is no clear-cut picture of the person inclined toward suicide. The person who attempts suicide is sometimes a social outcast and sometimes the most popular person in the class. Sometimes it's a high achiever and sometimes it's a low achiever. Girls attempt suicide more often than boys, but boys more often succeed because they choose more lethal means. Below is a list of warning signs or red flags that may indicate a vulnerability to suicide. However, many of these same symptoms could also be indications of *other* adolescent problems.

Ten Warning Signs

1. Talking about suicide. Probably seventy to eighty percent of suicide victims have mentioned it in some way beforehand.

2. A change in interests. The person may no longer care about a hobby or school or physical appearance.

3. Isolation from other people.

4. Writing poems or drawing pictures about death.

5. An upbeat mood after a period of depression. Sometimes after the anguish of the indecision about going through with suicide people become happy and peaceful once they resolve to do so.

6. Giving away cherished objects.

7. Obtaining a gun, pills, a knife, a rope, etc.

8. Changes in patterns of sleeping and eating.

9. Use of drugs and alcohol. Many teen suicides occur under the influence of alcohol or some other drug, which blurs the judgment and provides the courage to go through with the action.

10. A person who has coped adequately with a series of crises suddenly has a new problem on top of all the others.

Recent research on suicide has shown that a significant number of teenage suicides are due to confusion over sexual identity. A teen who believes himself to be gay (or believes herself to be a lesbian) may feel more ostracized than the member of any other group. Homosexuality is a threatening topic to young people working out their own identities. These young people are so terrified by the lack of acceptance in their homes, peer culture or even among their friends that they feel they have to resort to ending their lives. This is a sad commentary on our ability to accept others as they are.

Remember that a veiled threat, an indirect remark or a bold assertion may all be cries for help. Only part of a suicidal person wants to die; part wants to live. That's why suicidal people give warnings. They don't really want to die; they want to eliminate some problem from their life. Teenage thoughts about suicide have a strange dimension. Many imagine that others will be sorry once they're gone and that they will be able to witness or overhear that sorrow. This is false. They will have no awareness of what others are saying and feeling.

Some teen suicides happen subconsciously. An example of this is a young person who breaks up with his girlfriend and then drives a hundred miles an hour down a dark road and ends up hitting a pole and killing himself. Many teenage accidents that occur when only one person is in the vehicle are thought to be suicides.

Always take a suicide threat seriously. It's better to be

too cautious than to let a remark go. Always tell others who can help this person (usually a parent), who are around them all the time. *Never keep threats of suicide confidential.* It's better to lose a friendship than a friend.

Teenage Suicide: Thirteen Deadly Myths

1. **Nothing could have stopped her once she decided to kill herself.**
2. **The person who fails at suicide the first time will eventually succeed.**
3. **People who talk about killing themselves never do.**
4. **When he talks about killing himself, he's just looking for attention. Ignoring him is the best thing to do.**
5. **Talking about suicide to a troubled person may give him morbid ideas.**
6. **People under a psychiatrist's care rarely commit suicide.**
7. **Suicides often occur out of the blue.**
8. **People who kill themselves are insane.**
9. **Once a person tries to kill himself and fails, the excruciating pain and shame will keep him from trying again.**
10. **Once the depression seems to be lifting, would-be suicides are out of danger.**
11. **Only a certain type of youngster commits suicide and my child just isn't the type.**
12. **Suicides are mainly old people with only a few years left to live.**
13. **Suicides run in families, so you can't do much to prevent it.**

From *A Cry For Help*, Dr. Mary Griffin and Carol Felsenthal (Garden City, N.Y.: Doubleday and Co., 1983)

This personal reflection on suicide was shared with me recently by one of my students. It's a true story.

> Suicide is one of the main causes of death of teens today. I might not know a lot about suicide in the area of statistics or facts, but I feel I do know a lot about it

from experience and from a teen's point of view. What I have to say about suicide is from my own experience and the reasons why I did it.

For the past two years I have had problems, problems with my family, friends, school, and problems that were invisible to even myself. I used to get pains in my stomach and I never knew why. On the outside I was this popular cheerleader, Homecoming Queen, with a lot of friends. But inside I was a sensitive, scared and quiet person. I felt as if the world was out to get me, and in order to protect myself I had to seclude myself or find another way out.

I found out the pains in my stomach were ulcers. When the doctor asked if I had a lot of stress I said, "No." He talked to my parents and they denied it too. They thought my life was just great the way everyone else did. Things started to really fall apart the week before February vacation. The ulcers were worse and my friends seemed to turn on me along with my boyfriend dumping me. The last source I had was a close friend I had for a few years. I tried to tell him, but when he turned, too, I broke down.

I wanted to leave the world temporarily and just get away. The way out I chose was suicide. If my attempt had worked, it would have been a long term solution to a short-term problem. I swallowed forty-three Advil, and what I had to go through from that point on was worse than any problem I had ever previously experienced. I had tubes up my nose, my body was violated and people never left me alone.

That incident made me see for the first time just how important my life really was. I was happy to be alive and realized that I would never want to go through that again. I began to see a psychologist, and she helped me to deal with my problems and realize that there is a way out, and it doesn't mean suicide. It's just simply letting your feelings out. It's OK to break down and to let people know that you're not perfect.

I know a lot of things now that I didn't know before. I guess God was trying to tell me that my time on earth wasn't up yet. I just hope someday that I can get up enough courage to tell my story, because there's nothing in the world I would like more than to help others who are in situations like I was. It's so important to let them know that there are other ways out.

Nadine, age 17